GUITARS

SANDBAGS

AND SAIGON TEA

GUITARS

SANDBAGS

AND SAIGON TEA

Poems, Thoughts, and Memories

THURMAN P. WOODFORK

Table of Contents

ISBN 978-0-6151-6456-4

Author's Note: While the poems in this book are mostly works of fiction written for and about others, the anecdotes generally reflect my own experiences as I remember them. T. P. Woodfork

ISBN 978-0-6151-6456-4

I Was in Vietnam Last Night

I was in Vietnam last night;
I know, for when I awoke, I had cried.
I suppose the reason was because
 someone I knew had died.

The thoughts I'd kept at bay all day
grew like noxious weeds and bloomed,
and the aroma that they gave off
carried the scent of impending doom:

The smell of rotting jungle plants,
the pungent odor of *nouc mam,*
the acrid stink of powder smoke,
mingled with the reek of napalm,

slowly filled my nostrils
as memories were evoked
of firefights, Dustoffs, air strikes,
and drifting, colored smoke...

I heard a guitar softly strummed;
 I was holding a rusty can of beer.
For a time the war faded back a bit,

along with the ever-present fear.

My thoughts shifted across the seas
to that other life I knew:
tinkering with cars, going on dates,
and hanging out drinking brew.

I wondered if I could ever be part
of those carefree days once again,
when thoughts of death never crossed
my mind...I was immortal then.

It seems I grew up all at once,
learned things I never wanted to know;
last night old ghosts came drifting back,
like softly falling snow...

And they chilled the nighttime hours
when I should've been sound asleep,
crept into my ears, stole up my nose,
and caused my eyes to weep.

I was in Vietnam last night,
where my youth suddenly came to an end.
Along with peace and tranquility,
and some very special friends.

*~For my friends Dave Stevenson, Chuck
Schwiderski,
and Ray Greiner, who sometimes travel afar at night.*
~~~

Who Knows Why?

How often have I asked myself
why it is that I'm still here?
Why did that damned bullet just
barely graze my ear?

Ol' Moby, who was behind me,
probably thinking about his farm,
gave a grunt and slumped right
over, grabbing out for my arm.

His eyes were wide and puzzled
as he lay there on the ground.
Then, they just sort of went out;
he was gone without a sound.

I found myself down beside him
clutching him in that muddy hole,
though the sniper didn't fire again;
he was satisfied with one soul.

But in my heart was a dagger
he had buried clear to the hilt;
and for all the days that remain
to me I'll carry a nagging guilt.

I know full well that it ain't my
fault, but I'll remember to the end
how that bullet whipped right past
my head and drilled into my friend.

And not a single word can be said
that will take away my pain,
nor all the wishes in the world
bring Moby back again.

So I'm left to grieve and wonder
why it came to be that night
that Moby's eyes and not mine
dimmed and lost their light.

It wasn't because I was smarter,
a lot braver, or more bold;
and I sure ain't built no empires
or saved a thousand souls.

The only reason I can think of
why it's him and not me that's dead,
is because, at just the right second,
I simply turned my head.
~~~

A Smile, A Hope

The heartbreak of such a young lad trying to smile, with his eyes so sad that they cause my heart to slow its beat as I look upon his youthful face, too innocent, it would seem, to have a place in something as mean and cruel as war. I wonder what he thought he was fighting for?

Did he volunteer, or was he drafted? Did he feel heroic...or merely shafted? When I went to war, I was thirty-one; he looks almost young enough to have been my son, thinking of things like proms instead of how to avoid enemy bombs, and survive in the lethal jungles of Vietnam.

That he was weary is clear to be seen. How long had he been living out in 'The Green'? Hunting and being hunted 'til his nerves stretched thin and the ghost of a smile that had once been a grin was all that remained of the youth within.

Did the growing somberness in his eyes finally smother that smile until it died? Did the insidious inhumanity inherent in war change and harden him even more until he became a reflexive machine adapting to cope with the treacherous 'Green'?

If he did manage to survive the war and return to his home once more; in time was he able to revive that grin until it wreathed his face once again from laughing eyes to the tip of his chin? I hope and pray that really came true: I wish I knew; I wish I knew....

Remember

Was it years ago or only yesterday I walked
into eternity and forever became
Part of this place where my comrades and I
Lie lifeless, unmoving, slain?

It seemed in one savage, red explosion we
Were ambushed, surrounded, dead.
The jungle returned to its ancient business,
Assimilating us while our bodies still bled.

We all knew that brave motto about no one
Ever being left behind;
But, in spite of good intentions, one cannot
Retrieve what one cannot find.

So, here we lie violated, stripped, fodder for
The jungle's insatiable appetite.
Slowly returning to the earth as time rolls on,
Days rotating endlessly into nights.

But, console yourself, for I really am not in
This place where my body fell.
It only took an instant before I was divested
Of that confining shell.

I live in the abiding love tenderly shining forth
when my picture is caressed by your eyes;
I'm part of the gentle breath released when
You think of me and sigh.

I am there in the crinkled curve of your lips
when, after a while,
The memories of our happy times together
cause you to pause and smile.

I exist in the sad tears that slowly well
When thoughts of me make you cry;
As long as you remember - as you hold
Me in your heart - I cannot die.

Do not forget me, Father; fold me forever
In the warmth of your mind, Mother.
And you, Little Sister, I know you'll always
Cherish the memory of your brother.

I am forever here with you … Remember.
~~~

Faye Sizemore – wife of a former Marine

The Unseen Warrior

No, you need not have fought in
Vietnam, or the other wars,
To suffer from the enduring pain
They've inflicted upon the poor
Unseen victims of their horror.

How many nights have you spent,
Filled with a deep, aching sorrow,
As your veteran tossed and moaned
In distress that stole tomorrow?

You both relive those battles again;
You've both felt the fear and pain
As comrades fell and bullets flew...
Red blood flowed, fresh and new...
You might as well have been there, too.

Although you never in person saw
The awful scenes from that war,
It's held you, wounded, in its claw,
Tried to gulp you down its maw.

These words are certain and true,
For you have paid a wealth of dues;
There are no combat medals for you,
But, oh, My Love, you've lived it, too.

Inspired by Melanie C. Campos' poem
"Never Fought in 'Nam"
~~~

Trust

The unquestioning trust in a small child's eyes;
The gentle, warm trust in a lover's sighs,
The essential trust of soldiers in each other,
Strong and vital as that between brothers.

Trust in all its many manifestations
Forms the bedrock of lasting relations.
Trust that's enduring and eternally steadfast
Nourishes and protects a love that will last

Through all the travails that life has to give,
Easing the journey for as long as one lives.
Trust is quiet and self-effacing
And does not set the heart to racing;

It has no need of flamboyant speech,
Does not force one to kneel or beseech.
Trust doesn't require a fervent prayer,
For, unless betrayed, it is always there.
~~~

Memorial Day Memories

Memorial Day and memories,
A time for somber reflection...
So it would seem. But my unruly
Mind wanders in its own direction.

When I look at my brother's picture,
He in his graduation cap and gown,
Hanging all those years on the wall,
I'm not moved to a mournful frown.

It isn't his death that comes to mind
When my eyes rest upon him there;
It's the joy he brought in his short life,
The caring and the love he shared.

And Vietnam – it isn't just visions
Of pain, and of death, and war;
It wasn't always Bombs and Blood
During my stay in old III Corps.

We perched up on the sand bags,
Swapped lies and sang some songs,
And we built a few warm memories
That still are holding strong.

I remember Liar's Dice one time,
And a wild trip into Tay Ninh
To the Green Door in the wee hours,
And the trouble we'd have been in

Had Top or the VC intercepted us
As we made our tipsy flight
Down dark roads on a crazy whim
In Top's 'borrowed' jeep that night.

My mind touches on friends I made
During those happy years in Spain,
Though some have passed from this
Life, their memories bring no pain.

Yes, I've spent time in a place or two,
And I've met a lot of folks.
In truth, I didn't like every one; it
Wasn't all sunshine and jokes.

But it's the camaraderie I recall, the
Card games, the harmony, the pranks.
I mostly remember the pleasant times,
With gratitude, and with thanks.

~~~

All My Bright Tomorrows

I lie there looking up into the sweaty face of the
medic leaning over me. I'm surprised how much he
looks like my father. But that can't be; I never
noticed the resemblance before. Besides, I'm twenty,
and Doc's only twenty-five.

I remember a particular picture of my father, bare-
chested, wearing shower clogs and jungle fatigue
pants, taking a short break from his own war. Except

that Dad was smiling then, he had looked very much like this weary, concerned friend gazing down at me now with so much pain in his eyes. Funny I'd never noticed before...maybe it's the painkillers playing tricks with my mind.

"Doc?" I must not have spoken as loudly as I thought, because he leans closer, as if to hear me better. "What is it, Buddy," he asks gently, smiling now. The smile doesn't quite reach his eyes; the pain and concern remain there. "Am I going to make it?"

"Sure," he says reassuringly. "You got my personal guarantee." I'm very tired, so I close my eyes momentarily. Doc says, rather sharply, "Stay awake, 'Oscar'; the chopper's almost here." He seems to wince slightly as he says my nickname. I know he's telling the truth about the chopper because I can hear it in the near distance, the sound of its rotors growing steadily louder. I sigh, and he speaks again, still gently reassuring, "Don't worry, you're gonna make it; everything's gonna be fine." He touches my right shoulder; "You hear me, Partner?"

"I hear you, Doc," I say, as the Medevac chopper sets down close by. It's suddenly important that I try to make him feel better; it's probably because of the pain in his eyes. He's dry-eyed, but I know the tears must be running down inside him. I look up into those eyes once again, and then down at the bloody bandages covering my torso and hiding the mangled mess that's what's left of my left hand and lower left arm.

I wonder if a one-armed jazz pianist can make it to the big time. Despite the medication, I feel a far off sadness beginning to grow in me as realization slowly overcomes hope. Doc will have to find a new pianist for our quartet. Oscar Peterson's rep is safe.

For Bruce 'Doc' Melson,
and all his brethren.

That Old Feeling

The years of self-medication
Haven't erased a single scene;
Rifle fire and exploding mortars
Still echo through his dreams.

Shadows move in the darkness
Whenever his eyes are closed,
The remembered stench of
Violent death violates his nose.

He still sees Short Round's mouth
Stretched in the awful scream
That penetrated straight to his soul,
And froze his blood, it seemed.

Once again the slow pulsing
Of suppressed, smoldering rage
Simmers deep within him,
Coiled and waiting in its cage.

The years quietly creep on by,
His malaise has steadily grown,
While discontent keeps building,
Poisoning what peace he's known.

Ghostly voices, whispering, seem
To plead, calling his name;
He feels the old twinges of guilt
Though he knows he can't be blamed

for old friends who lie forever still,
While he sits cradling his drink.
He slowly lifts it to his lips
In a futile effort not to think.

"Rest in Peace," he almost pleads
In a silent, heartfelt toast;
The bartender sighs and leaves him be,
To commune alone with his ghosts.

Now I Lay Me Down...

When the aching within me builds in
the indifferent silences of the night,
When unexpressed sorrow escapes from
dark corners of my mind into the light,
When 'Should I have?' and 'Could I have?'
begin anew their damnable play,
Who is there to listen? Who hears
or pays attention to what I say?
When years of regret and longing rise,
roiling unchecked through my soul,
When all those clear-as-yesterday memories
run rampant, seething hot - then cold,
When old guilt and anger reassert their
agitation and once again hold sway,
who truly gives a damn? Who is there
who cares enough to forgive me
...if, indeed, I could pray?
~~~

Too Much 'Self-Restraint'

There are many things that bother me,
I'm filled with sadness and ennui,
And deeper pain that you can't see;
My soul is begging, "Set me free."

But something in me says, "Oh no,
I'll never, ever let you go;
I need your sorrow so I can grow,
Your constant pain is my life's flow."

I look around with jaded eyes
At all the things that life denies,
As all the while my heart still cries
Vainly reaching toward the skies.

There must be better things for me;
If I could bring myself to agree
And rise up from my aching knees,
I could set my spirit free.

If I found strength within my heart,
To step across my own ramparts,
And draw myself a new life's chart,
Rebirth would have a chance to start.

Of all the enemies I have found
That try to chain me to the ground,
Keep me blind, gagged, and bound
Only one could ever hold me down:

The demon that is mostly me
Nurtures the pain that you can't see.
It refuses to leave and let me be;
It keeps my soul crying, "Set Me Free!"

Dedicated to Gil Lewis
~~~

In Our Hearts

We carry them in our
hearts, souls, minds;
physically buried, but
never left behind...
Remembered, cherished
until our own earthly end.
Comrades, brothers,
companions, friends...
Death's final embrace
flouted and denied.
Their essences live
within us, deep inside...
While we breathe,
they have not died.
~~~

NUI BA DEN THE "BLACK VIRGIN" MOUNTAIN, TAY NINH PROVINCE
SEEN FROM DKT 7, 819TH TCB - 'PENTHOUSE' 1966-1967

Friendships and Departures

I'm standing alone in the aromatic darkness of Trang-Sup, gazing off to where Nui Ba Den looms dimly against the starry sky. The muted noises of the camp go on behind me. And, as always, the almost subliminal rumbling of continual bombardments underlies the background of camp sounds. Some guys in the little club, backed by a pretty good guitar player, are singing their own version of the Ballad of the Green Berets. Barry Sadler never thought up those words.

Something rustles faintly off to one side near the sandbags. I suddenly remember that I'm standing alone in the dark, and that I hate snakes, although I don't think (hopefully) that a snake would be making any noise. I decide it's probably a foraging rat and briefly wonder where Tu Do is. Tu Do is one of the camp mascots, a medium size, nondescript, black-and-white mutt that dearly loves to chase and kill rats. You only have to point one out to her and she's off after it like a shot.

Why am I out here by myself, communing with the spirit of the Black Virgin that dwells inside Nui Ba Den? It's because my friend Larry shipped out today. There's not even the satisfaction of knowing that he's returning safely home, since he didn't go home. He just moved on to another A Team camp. Somebody noted that the last three camps Larry had been on were overrun shortly after he departed. Now, there's a pleasant thought to contemplate.

[Fortunately, Trang-Sup broke that string of bad luck; its walls remained intact and unbreached during its American occupation. Finally, the Air Force detachment was deactivated in the spring of '68, and then the Special Forces A Team left sometime later. Det. 7 and A-301 ceased to exist. I had been gone for nearly a year when the American presence on Trang-Sup began to end. I had gone to Clark Air Force Base in the Philippines. Gone, but not forgotten. I had the signal honor of being in charge of the crew that was sent to retrieve the Air Force electronic equipment from Trang-Sup after Detachment 7 was deactivated. Obviously, I had not moved far enough away. When my old hooch mate introduced me to the Air Force Commander, the CO said, "Ah, the notorious Sergeant Woodfork!" as he was shaking my hand. I decided not to ask what he meant.]

"Don't form close attachments," they said; it would be too painful should a friend be killed. True enough, perhaps, but Larry is very much alive, just gone somewhere else in Vietnam. Anyway, does anybody ever really fully observe that supposed taboo? In later years, after listening to 'Nam vets talk about their friends and experiences, I definitely doubt it.

I doubt it even while I'm still in Vietnam. There's the indelible memory of some of the Special Forces guys on Trang-Sup weeping in anger and frustration while they listen to the radio as another A Team camp desperately fights to keep from being overrun. Most of them had served with the people in that camp at one time or another. These seasoned troops were not shedding tears for casual acquaintances. They identified closely with those men.

As for me, I would have thought that I had long ago become inured to the departure, if not the death, of friends. After all, I had spent years on remote radar sites, where people came and went almost constantly. Most Air Force people don't go PCS in units; we move about singly, particularly among small radar squadrons like the ones I was always part of. I certainly should have been used to losing friends to redeployment.

I stand there gazing into the humid night, wondering if there's really something extra special about friendships formed in a war zone. In spite of the caveats against it, do we become closer, form a special bond, because of the circumstances of our shared existence in constant danger? That danger is always there, regardless of where we happen to be, or what we are doing. I wonder...does it hurt as much, does the pain last as long, if a friend is killed away from your sight and hearing?

Hell, I'm no philosopher; I don't know. So I give it up, leaving Nui Ba Den to the perennially surrounded Americans in the radio relay station on its summit and the VC infesting its slopes. I go in to join the singing in the club: "Jesus was a lifeguard at the Third Army pool, Jesus was a lifeguard at the Third Army pool, Jesus was a lifeguard at the Third Army pool – Jesus saves, Jesus saves, Jesus saves."
~~

See Puff Fly

See Puff. See Puff fly.
Oops! You can't see Puff
in that Stygian sky...

But you can see his
fiery breath

as he exhales
crimson death
on the attackers
gathered below.
No wonder that
we loved him so!
~~~

The Wall
(to Demonstrators)

How much more do you want of us? We wait here in dismay as you plan to disrupt our serenity, your placards screaming of 'Peace'. Don't you know there is no war here – only blessed release from the pain and agony of our journey to this hallowed place? Don't sully it with your anger – do not demean it with your slogans. Here, there is commiseration, not turmoil, solace, not confrontation. Take your anger to those who caused it. There is no place for it here. We have endured enough. Leave us to commune in harmony with our comrades on both sides of our Wall – those who have passed through, and those who wait to complete the journey. Please do not misunderstand; we may have arrived here as the result of war and violence, but we have transformed this Wall into a place of eternal love. Let our repose remain inviolate for as long as this nation endures. Grant us the peace you demand.
~~~

Childish Things
 Children, ah, children
- the hope of us all;
I've watched them die,
or sicken and crawl
on African plains
under carrion birds' eyes
while uncaring politicians
postured and lied.

I've seen them fleeing
from war birds' dives,
dodging and scrambling
in fear of their lives.
I've seen them take
a few lives of their own,
wielding a weapon
as if they were grown...

Or hurl a grenade
with murderous aim
as though engaged
in some deadly game
where the object was
to slaughter and maim,
and not amusement,
applause, or fame.

They'll turn themselves
into walking bombs
and become 'martyrs'
in order to harm
people they shouldn't
be old enough to hate...
On such shoulders
rests our ultimate fate.

How did we permit
such a huge culture gap?
what can we do before
it all comes unwrapped
and leads to the long-
promised fiery end -
Something as simple
as truly being friends?
~~~

The Eyes

The stony eyes of a young 'Nam grunt
Have the gaze of a man too long in the hunt.
Aged eyes unblinking in that still young face
Looking straight at you with never a trace

Of emotion or laughter, apparently unfeeling;
Eyes of a soul that'll be a long time healing
From all the things that he's seen and done...
The many places fought over and won...

Then abandoned only to be fought for again;
So what if the cost was a few of his friends?
Or was it just about an entire platoon
That bled and died in that damned monsoon?

The weary days merged into soggy nights
Punctuated by murderous firefights,
And all the while his eyes slowly aged
As deep inside grew a smoldering rage

That might not erupt for years and years
Or perhaps only turn into bitter tears
That try to wash away aching thoughts -
Piercing memories of harsh battles fought -

Memories drowsing deep within his brain
Waiting to be roused by the sound of rain.
Did the years ever soften those frigid eyes?
Or did they turn inward toward the cries

Of brothers who fell while mourning skies wept
And death came quietly or noisily leapt
Through chaos and fury to bear away
Fallen comrades from the bloody fray?

I hope one day those jaded eyes close
In dreamless sleep and peaceful repose
As vivid memories slowly fade and dim,
Allowing those eyes to smile once again.

Solitude...
touched by
lassitude
...mind
gone drifting
far away
caught up in
a distant day
inky brooding
foreboding sky
living silence
stifled sigh
sandbags grey
in humid night
waiting for
revealing light
finally there's the
welcome dawn
another night
lived and gone
better yet
you also know
there's one less
day left to go.

Always, They Came

They always came in answer to the call;
Day or night, they gave their all
In a fiercely earnest dash with death,
Racing to arrive while there was still breath
In men who were yesterday's boys...
Whose eyes had lost their joy...
Whether they were 'Dustoff' or 'Medevac'
Wasn't important to the men they took back.
As the saying goes, "What's in a name?"
It was enough that, when called, they came.
~~~

The Hill

Roberta Flack is softly singing, "He was strummin'
my pain...yeah, he was singin' my life..." And, like a
waking dream, as if summoned by the music, it all
comes drifting back again–

Ron starts wearily up that same old hill, eyes intent,
walking carefully, his senses alert. At an odd noise,
long dormant feral instincts kick in and he feels his
ears twitch as they try to swivel and pinpoint the
sound.

"My God," he thinks ruefully to himself, "I really am
becoming an animal." It's the third time they've
climbed this particular hill, but familiarity has not
bred contempt. He knows who's waiting somewhere
up on those heavily forested slopes; he can feel
their eyes on him. No wonder his ears twitch.

He moves steadily on, keeping his distance,
following the grubby, slightly ragged figure ahead of
him as they warily climb higher and higher through
the green gloom. They've been in the field for days.
Sweat starts to form under his helmet and run into
eyes. He brushes it away with an impatient swipe.

No time for blurred vision.

As he takes another step, shots suddenly ring out, and a blow slams into his hip, jerking him off stride. He hits the ground and rolls over onto his unhurt side. "Well, I'll be damned!" he thinks, as he tries to gasp air back into his shocked lungs. Something wet is running over his throbbing hip, and he doesn't want to look.

Finally, he does, and sees the water trickling from his punctured canteen, which has been twisted around almost completely behind him.

He keeps still, breathing deeply for a moment, as bullets whip through the air all around him. Then, anger boils up, red and hot, and he fires into the dark foliage off to his right, hoping to hit something, anything. The firing stops as suddenly as it began, and he lies there, cursing softly to himself.

Turner, who had been trailing Ron and saw him twist and go down, crawls up to him. Seeing the dark, wet stain spreading down Ron's pants leg, Turner exclaims, "You've been hit, man!"

At that, Ron starts to laugh, a little bit hysterically. Turner thinks he's going into shock; Ron sobers at the concern showing through the dirt on his friend's sweaty face and shakes his head. "No," he says, "but you'll have to share your water with me." He shows Turner the ruined canteen, and they both start to laugh with the release of tension.

Turner rises to his knees, then his head jerks oddly and he falls backwards in an awkward sprawl. He lies motionless on the ground as blood slowly wells out of the hole where his right eye had been.

The memory of that single shot hangs heavily on the muggy air. For a split second, there is no other sound. Then Ron drops the canteen, screaming for Doc, knowing full well it's useless.

He shakes his head abruptly and pushes the 'Stop'

button on the remote as Roberta croons, "He sang
as if he knew me, in all my dark despair..."

The music stops, but the memories play on.
Another Veterans' Day Nears
~~~

Brothers Mine

Brothers, brothers, where'd you go?
Off to heaven and left me below
Full of sorrow unexpressed,
Alone and grieving, so bereft.

Though I often feel you near
I wish so much you were really here.
I miss the comradeship we shared,
The crazy things we sometimes dared.

There's a yearning in my soul
Where you once made it whole...
And some guilt that I still live
While you gave all there is to give.

But, surely as the sun brings dawn,
While I breathe, your memory lives on.
Search the world; you'll never find
A truer memorial than my mind.

For Bob Drury ~ BlueGhost Two-Zero
Troop F, 8th Cavalry (BlueGhost) Vietnam
May '69 - December '70
~~~

Peace

Our war there ended long ago,
Though memories linger still
Of bloody battles bitterly fought
Over once-important hills.

The craters are slowly healing
In the red, bomb-blasted earth,
While Agent Orange still remains,
Corrupting and sullying births.

Trams climb the placid slopes
Of brooding Nui Ba Den
But I recall the Viet Cong
Who once lurked deep within.

There are no Hueys in the skies,
Dragon Ships have ceased their roar,
No River Rats make perilous trips
Past grim and hostile shores.

Though peace has come to Vietnam
The years haven't been as kind
To the souls who still go on patrol
Through the jungles in their minds.
~~~

The Undefeated
I've come home, but not from War;
It waits there, near my mind's door.
I can hear it snuffling,
Its horny feet shuffling,
Waiting to possess me once more.

I'm afraid it will never relent,
My nostrils are filled with its scent.
It rumbles and growls,
And ceaselessly prowls,
Adding to my lasting torment.

It's just waiting for me to sleep,
So into my mind it can creep,
And bring back scenes,
I'd left in the 'Green',
Chortling as it watches me weep.

But I refuse to accept defeat;
I cannot and will not retreat.
I've done my best,
And, just like 'Beau Geste',
I still am one of the elite.

My duties I never will shirk;
I rise each weekday for work,
And try as it might,
I will win this fight
While deep in my brain it still lurks.

I know I'll conquer each day,
And that is how I will stay -
Let it snarl and groan,
Howl and moan,
Like a wolf in search of its prey -
Until Death comes to take me away.
For Charles 'Chuck' Schwiderski

When Robins Weep

When robins weep and sorrows creep
through minds with memories so sad,
do soldiers weep alone in their sleep
mourning old friends they once had?

They're so bereaved...their shoulders
heave as the bitter tears start to flow;
 how they grieve as thoughts reweave
bloody scenes from battles long ago.

Yes, they cry as friends again die
in jungles and heights far from home;
though streets may teem, in forlorn
dreams they feel so lost and alone.

So we must pray those yesterdays
will fade and finally drift away,
as welcome peace brings sweet
release and tomorrow a kinder day.

 - For Chuck 6/19/2006
~~~

Waking to Sadness

Though I've often felt loss before,
It never becomes easy to bear;
As another steps through life's door
I find it impossible not to care.

All the soothing sounds we make
All the platitudes we say,
Can't my quiet melancholy take
Nor lift the sadness of that day.

 As my life slowly unfolds
I'm sure that I will always find
Wistful thoughts from days of old
Gently coursing through my mind.

Tomorrow is the Fourth of July,
Was that dreaming sorrow for
Those genuine patriots who died
To protect these nurturing shores?

So many of us have put aside
Personal differences, anger, pain
Because of our national pride
And not for any selfish gain.

Not for red states, not for blue
Did we fight and bleed and strive;
It was not for some political hue
That we offered up our lives.

For friends fighting at our side,
Living embodiments of our land,
That is why we fought and died;
That is why we took that stand.

During tomorrow's celebrations,
When banners snap against the sky,
Remember those who preserved the nation;
Remember the patriots who bravely died.
~~~

Enemy's Dreams

I wonder how the former enemy copes,
now that our war is done;
does he suffer bouts of melancholy
or dream of battles lost and won?

Does a bone-deep mantle of depression
settle 'round him like a cape
as he eases his way through the jungles
of his mind seeking ways to escape

from the never-ending horror of
memories that will not fade?
Does he, too, mourn friends' bodies
lying lifeless in some glade?

And is his sleep troubled by the
shadowy, stalking shade
of an ageless soldier who pursues him
along a gloomy jungle path
or waits in ambush to trap him in a
deadly unleashing of wrath?

Is there a 'Wall of Heroes' that can
ease his mental pain
and slow the recollections that
march unbidden through his brain?

When the velvet night comes softly
to cloak the terrain from view,
does he stir uneasily in his sleep?
Could that demon in his dreams be you?
~~~

©David Honey

Journey

I'm weary; I seek a resting place.
I'm lonely; I need companionship.
My heart is sore; I require understanding.
My memories plague me; I must find peace.
But I don't know how to ask for these things.
Have I come to the right place?
Will my long journey finally end here?
Have I found what I've sought for so long,
Or is this another lovely, empty promise?
A theater with enticing, vacuous dialogue:
"I'm not an empathic person, but I play one here."
I cannot bear more disappointment;
Can't you feel my anguish?
One more hollow phrase will pierce me like a lance -
I will drown in this swirl of counterfeit caring
Like a helpless babe caught in a raging whirlpool.
Damn you; stop talking and listen!
Sense what I leave unexpressed.
You claim to have walked this path before me;
Can't you see through the bravado in my words?
Where is your insight and compassion?
I throb with sub-vocal cries for help;
I pulse with the need to reach out for support.

My eyes beseech even as I turn away...
But you do not discern my wordless plea...
You neither see nor hear the inner me.
I must move on.

Dedicated to the Veterans Administration
~~~

War Child

Oh, God, this is not the way
I had planned to end my day:
Facing me is a bright-eyed child,
Staring at me, tense and wild.

Time stops, the world seems calm,
But this boy is a ticking bomb,
Standing there in dappled shade,
Tightly clutching a hand grenade.

Does he fully understand
That he'll die if he lifts his hand?
He must know to move will send
Him straight to a bloody end.

I can't let him get too near;
If he moves, he'll trip the fear
Slowly building in my head
And I'll surely shoot him dead.

Sweet Jesus, can't he see
I have no choice – it's him or me,
I don't want to kill this child...
Dear God, he's starting to smile!

My hesitation makes him bold,
My whole body turns icy cold
As his hands start to lift...
On its own, my rifle shifts.

Then he steps from shade to sun;
In that instant, his life is done.
Another stone drops on my soul;
Suddenly, I feel very old.

~~~

Shuckin' and Jivin'

Lord, I'm weary and just a little dismayed, sometimes
even puzzled by what I see...Maybe the problem lies
with me. Even after all these years, expecting people to
mean what they say...

But so many use words like verbal makeup - just
another device to make the old persona seem better
than it is...a little linguistic eyeliner and rhetorical
rouge to cover up the blemishes, while in the
background, The Temptations can be heard softly
singing, "Rap on, Rapper, rap on..."

Promises made, promises broken, promises
implied and left unspoken. Another sort of lie.

And I have to wonder at the sycophants who never
look past the façade, who doggedly believe that mole
really is a beauty spot. Are they more to be pitied than
scorned?

Ah, well, as time goes on and the road narrows, are
such things even worth the time that's spent in
contemplation? Maybe, in the timeworn Nam phrase, it
really don't mean nothin'. At least, not anything worth
bothering about.

On second thought, maybe that's more cynicism than
dismay. Just idle thoughts on another crappy day...

~~~

Friendly Fire

The enemy is close, almost here -
Feeling trapped, filled with fear,
Men belly down in the jungle mire,
Trying to avoid the withering fire.

A giant steps, and steps again,
Supporting fire comes walking in.
A brief pause, then thunder and pain,
Leaves and branches fall like rain.

A number transposed or misheard,
In the excitement, a garbled word
Caused coordinates to be incorrect;
The air is filled with death and regret.

Charlie fades into the Green,
Dust-offs head for the bloody scene,
Hurrying forward to offer relief
From the carnage and rising grief.

Survivors wait and mentally damn
Another screwed-up day in the 'Nam.
~~~

Regret

Steeped in sorrow, drenched in tears,
Lacerated by lasting fears,
Phantoms ghosting through the night
Fill the heart with regret and fright.

Will this sorrow never end?
Won't the wounds ever mend?
Damned forever to a life of sighs,
Tortured memories and stifled cries.

How much longer must they pay?
Will these shadows forever stay,
Grisly reminders til life's last day?
Is there no litany that I can say?

I absorb the words that turn me cold
Yet burn my heart and sear my soul;
I clasp my arms, swaying to and fro -
Why is it they must suffer so?

I cannot watch this anymore,
And so, I start toward the door
And slowly move away from gloom,
But pause a moment, still in the room.

With hands half lifted in despair,
I offer up a fervent prayer
For restless spirits moving there.
It hangs, forlorn, in the brooding air.
~~~

Lyman Rigby

The Light Barrier

Lying here alone in the night,
Waiting wearily for the dawn,
Not reading, avoiding thinking,
And the lights are always on.

I don't really remember when
This particular habit began,
But I know it wasn't something
That I learned in the Nam.

I certainly didn't deliberately sit
Bathed in revealing light -
Not if I wanted to go on living
Through the deadly, ominous nights.

Now I lie here wide awake
Waiting quietly for the day,
While bright barriers of light beams
Hold prowling shadows at bay.
~~~

Night Fright – Day Light

Fears from the past
that, in the day,
are by the light
held at bay,

are freed to roam
through shadowy gloom
when revealing light
has left the room.

The mind is not
distracted then
by the affairs
of mortal men.

Memories we wish
had never been born
people the night
until the morn.

Then welcome rays
from the rising sun
chase them back to
where they'd begun:

back to their caves
of remembered pain
to lurk there in shadow
'til night falls again.

Parent and Child

The concern of mothers and fathers
for sons and daughters at war,
is something some of the population
seems to have little compassion for.

"They're slow to send their heart's delight
to defend the homeland's shores?
Don't they know their child couldn't fight
for any more noble a cause?"

"It is my country, right or wrong,"
comes the proud, exultant cry.
"How can they deny their precious
child this glorious chance to die?"

What must parents feel when sending their child off to war? I can't imagine the intense, conflicting emotions that must pass through their minds.

Here is this child, this precious treasure that they have nurtured and cared for since infancy. An integral part of their lives, this very unique person they have guided, guarded and loved for so many years, is now moving on to what might be a grisly end or perhaps grave injury.

Maybe letters, calls, videos - all communication - will suddenly cease and they will never see or hear from this beloved child ever again. They're left to wonder what became of their child for the rest of their lives. What a cheery thought to contemplate at any time.

And yet, they must feel some measure of pride along with the fear and trepidation. This child standing before them is about to begin a reversal of roles of sorts – now, they are poised to become the protector, the barrier against harm to home and country. So the parents cloak their fear and project their pride.

Even if the child returns apparently whole and
healthy in body, what maladies may linger inside,
incubating and eating away undetected? What
demons may have slipped into the psyche, to turn
innermost thoughts into living hell?

Hopefully, he – or she – will be among those who
weather this ultimate of life-altering experiences
relatively unscathed and return to pick up their lives
where they left off. God willing, they will have a new
maturity and insight that will stand them in good
stead through the years to come.

Many others have passed through the flames to
come out the other side whole and intact in mind
and body. I would imagine that each parent is
fervently praying that their child will be counted
among that number.

Finally, and not to be forgotten, what of the children
who have to watch their parents go off to war? What
terrible images and unspoken fears, fueled by
movies and TV, must come to live in their young and
fertile imaginations? One can only wonder
~~~

Why?

The measuring sands whisper
as your life is slipping by;
 the anthems of your being
 become a murmured sigh.
 The sun inexorably lowers
in your twilight darkened sky,
while echoes grow ever fainter
from agonized, anguished cries
and brave friends all around you
fall broken to the earth and die.
You ask with your final breath,
"Please Lord, tell me: Why?"
© Copyright 1/23/2006
Thurman P. Woodfork

The Faithful Patriot
(or Sing a Song of Chicken Hawks)

Ah, you quick-witted verbal artist,
You master of the cogent phrase;
How deftly you weave your magic
As you mesmerize and amaze

While persuading the disinclined
With the magic of your words.
I swear I smell sunlit meadows
And hear sweetly singing birds

In spite of the leafless branches
And hint of snow on the wind;
You conjure the smell of roses
As though it were Spring again.

Your speech, so skillfully formed
And voiced in ringing tones,
Could make one rush to battle
Armed only with sticks and stones.

But, of course, you must stay behind,
Remaining True to The Cause,
Pumping out that fiery rhetoric
To rounds of patriotic applause.

Even though forced to remain at home
(Safe near your own front stoop)
You keep urging on the Faithful
To rally and 'Support The Troops'.

What would we do without you
As you work so tirelessly?
You're a paragon of selflessness,
Allegiance and Fidelity.

But, what if some of your relatives
Took a little part in the fray?
Maybe more vets could get back home,
Before they're blown away.

Oh, but you really do work too hard
To quibble over so small a thing;
Think of all the backing for the troops
Your unflagging cheerleading brings.

So go on with your work, brother
Boost that support ever stronger;
As the troops go on bleeding and dying,
And hoping this won't last much longer.
~~~

Remorse

I hear a familiar voice calling,
Calling from the used-to-be.
I feel a guitar softly thrumming
Serenades deep inside of me.

The chords vibrating within me
Summon dreams of long ago
Flowing down yearning years
With a longing that pains me so.

So why did I walk away
from what I hungered for?
Why did I pretend not to care
As I quietly closed that door?

All she ever asked was that
I return a modest part
Of the generous love she offered
From a free and open heart

Had I followed my true desire
I'd never have gone to war
And added such a burden
To a heart already sore

No standing watching helplessly
As people died in flames
No learning cold, hard lessons
Why war is not a game.

But, no, I had to go my way
Searching on distant shores
To find, aching years later,
I'd had all I needed, and more.

Memories of that lost love
are smothered by agonized cries
As shrieks from burning villagers
Drown out my lover's sighs.

I don't often think this way...
My soul can't bear the pain...
And only very briefly
Do I allow that strummed refrain

To pulse ever so gently
Behind my shuttered eyes
To a counterpoint of mortars
And a lover's long lost sighs.
~~~

The Hold

Caught in the coils of PTSD,
Secret thoughts clasped close to me
And locked forever deep inside;
As if by a kind of tortured pride.

I don't think you can understand
What sears my being like a brand
Etched layers deep into my soul,
Burnt there by War's fiery coals.

Lurid nightmares that end in tears,
Conjured up from deep-seated fears,
Live in memories decades old...
Haunting stories I have never told.

Dismaying, shifting changes of mood,
From laughter to a dark-hued brood,
Cause loved ones to shy away,
Uncertain how I'll react today.

How many times have I stepped back
From that abyss, so deep and black,
To resume my life and carry on
While wishing that I had gone

Down toward that beckoning release,
The enticing promise of Final Peace?
But something holds me in this life,
Despite the pain and ceaseless strife.

It's all the love I can see
Deep in your eyes reaching out to me...
Infusing me with eternal hope
That, if I learn to really cope

With the demons that beleaguer me,
The day will come when we're both free
To bask in the warmth of our love's sun
United forever together as one.

~~

The First, Last, (and only) Liberal G.I.

It sounds remarkable, but can it truly be that the only
Liberal who ever served in the U.S. military was me?
Those other guys must have been pulling my leg
when they claimed to be Libs. Even my own sibs!
Guess they just didn't want me to feel too lonely
should I discover that I was the one and only card-
carrying Liberal who ever learned to salute. Well,
shoot...not with a gun, I mean, I wouldn't want to be
a galoot about it or run around waving flags and
stuff. I always thought just being there and doing my
job was enough. Sort of ticks me off though, that my
brothers put me on for all those years. Hiding their
Conservative views for fear I might've begun to nag
if they'd wrapped themselves in the Flag and started

to pontificate. Rather makes me feel like an ingrate for not being aware of such extreme caring. Oh, how they must have longed to be wearing the Red, White, and Blue tastefully draped about their shoulders! But, being older, I guess they got used to catering to "The Brat"...we can blame Mama for that..."Look out for your little brother," she'd say, and they'd start to mumble, but not loud enough for her to hear them grumble. It's truly strange to discover the sacrifices of my brothers, and the reason there was never another. (Liberal in the military, that is.) And I only made it because my brothers were afraid of our dear, sweet old Mother!

~~~

Once More Among the Monuments

Washington, DC - indeed, the entire country - is full of monuments to one war or another. We excel in erecting impressive marble stones and grand, granite edifices in memory of our perished warriors.

They stand in tribute to the sacrifices of sisters and brothers who were caught up in and killed by the vast, insatiable, unyielding rapaciousness of war. They're symbolic of the thanks of a grateful nation.

The irony of it all is that so many of the earnest mourners who come to extol the heroic deeds and offer praise for the sacrifices of the fallen and their wounded fellows also seem to have learned little from the past.

Too many equate patriotism with blind faith in the words of our national leaders. We ignore Doctor Johnson's observation that, "Patriotism is the last refuge of the scoundrel."

In spite of the lessons of the past, we seem all too unaware that among these leaders are those who would deliberately guide us into war for reasons that will not stand up in the cold, clear light of objective examination free of all patriotic jingoism.

We are obligated to protect this country from _all_ of its enemies, both foreign and domestic.

We go on erecting statues and stones to honor those who suffer and perish in our 'just' wars, and weep over them as a consequence of our tendency to put emotion ahead of our reason.

We continue to send our kith and kin off into the unrelenting maelstrom of war in the name of God and Country. And we mourn for them among the cold, marble monuments.

Wouldn't it be marvelous if we were able to erect more memorials to peace than to war? What a shame that the world will never allow that dream to come to pass.
~~~

How NOT to Meet a General

After finishing my tour of duty in Vietnam, I transferred directly to Clark AFB in the Philippine Islands, where I remained for a month or so before taking a hop, Space Available, back to the States on leave. On the return trip to Clark, I got hung up in Japan, getting bumped repeatedly. It seems there was an extraordinary run of married officers hauling their families around SEA. Of course, they needed the seat more than I did, RHIP and all that, plus me being a single, raggedy-assed GI.

Anyway, when I saw I wasn't going to make it back to Clark on time, I checked in with the Security Police at the terminal, showed them my orders, and requested that they tell my squadron where I was and let them know that I'd probably be delayed. They said that they'd take care of it, and gave me a slip showing that I had reported to them.

I spent about another week reporting to the terminal, getting bumped, and heading back into town to enjoy the night life again. I even found a great soul food restaurant - greens, grits, and all. Not that I like grits, but that's another story. Anyway, I finally got a flight back to Clark and strolled into the barracks, nearly flat broke but content as hell. I was told to report to the commander yesterday. Apparently, they had people staking out my room to alert them if and when I showed up.

I trudged on over to the Orderly House and reported in as directed, only to have the Old Man demand to know where the hell I'd been. That sort of surprised me, since I figured the Security Police in Japan had advised the squadron where I was. Besides, somebody lower down the ladder usually took care of errant AWOLs.

Unbeknown to me, the SPs in Japan had not contacted my squadron. When I didn't report back from leave on time, the squadron called my house to find out where I was. I guess they figured that, once I finally got back to the States, I'd said to hell with SEA and decided to stay home and join Jody. When 5th Tac called my house looking for me, my mother, quite naturally, became concerned because she knew that I'd left in ample time to get back to Clark before my leave was up (IF I had taken a commercial flight). She didn't know anything about the uncertainties of 'Space A'.

However, what she did know was General Benjamin O. Davis' family, and she called them to find out if the good general could be prevailed upon to help her to locate her mysteriously vanished son. Since my luck was running that way, of course, the general was happy to oblige. It was my further good fortune that General Davis was then commanding 13th Air Force, which was headquartered, naturally, on Clark Air Force Base. He called over to my squadron and inquired as to my whereabouts, thereby stirring up quite a bit more interest on their part in locating me ASAP.

Of course, I was in Japan boozing it up, blissfully unaware that, not only was General Davis on the lovely island of Luzon, he was taking a personal interest in my activities. So, when I finally showed up on Clark, cheerfully worn out and sated, I found that the squadron brass was more than a little concerned about me. The first thing out of the CO's mouth was, "Where the hell have you been? General Davis has been calling here looking for you." This surprised me no end, since up until then, I'd had no idea General Davis was even aware of my existence.

I told the Old Man where I'd been and showed him the slip the SPs at the air terminal in Japan had given me to prove that I had made an effort to notify the squadron of my situation. The date showed that I had arrived in Japan four days before my leave was up. He took the slip and kept it, telling me that I could go back to the barracks and to be sure and call home: Mother Dear was worried. I heard nothing more about the matter from the squadron. I suppose that was due to the General's interest in my welfare.

Having discovered my mother's part in this little drama, I immediately phoned home and told her that I was fine and to check with the Red Cross if I ever disappeared again, not start bugging generals. General Davis, in particular, was not the type to view AWOL airmen with any degree of favor. Her reply was, "Well, he found you, didn't he?" I didn't bother to explain that nobody had found me; I'd managed to eventually wend my weary way back home all by my lonesome. Meanwhile, my commander had called Gen. Davis' office to tell him that the prodigal had finally returned, hung-over, but healthy.

One benefit from the whole flap was that the brass thought that the general and I were personal friends, not knowing that I had never so much as laid eyes on him in the flesh. Naturally, I made no effort to disabuse them of that notion.

Some months later, I did have the privilege of meeting General Davis when he inspected the shop on Lily Hill, where I was NCOIC at the time. He made no mention of my extended leave, but he did ask some pretty sharp questions about the equipment. Fortunately, I was long recovered from my hangover, because somebody had given him a very comprehensive briefing on the radar gear.

All in all, it was a felicitous ending to a well-deserved leave.

~~~

Epitaph

There is always time for tears,
Always time to remember,
Life is more than simply existing
From December to November.

It's all the things that we have done,
The good and all the bad;
Hopefully, it's remembering the good
That will make others sad

When I've finally ended my tour
Upon this fractious earth.
I can but hope, when my time ends,
I'll at least be worth

A tear or two of sorrow, a modicum
Of regret that my days are done,
That I no longer exist with you
Beneath the warming sun.

You must always remember this:
I may not be within your view,
But if there is an eternity,
I'll forever cherish you.

~~~

Inside the Wire

Sing a song of barbwire fences,
Things could go awry;
See the nervous GIs,
Hoping not to die.
Crouched behind the sand bags
Fighting off the dread,
Praying that the sunrise
Won't find us cold and dead.
Monsoon season's started,
Skies are wet and gray;
Won't be no sky-borne cavalry
Coming to save the day.
Tighten up the pucker string,
Throttle back the fear,
Tingling senses tell you,
Charlie's creeping near.
Mouth is just a little dry,
Jaws are clenched and tight;
Even hardcore atheists
Pray for morning light...
And something more
Than mortal help
To see us through this night.
~~~

Is it Memorial Day Again?

Sometime yesterday morning I read
Where somebody quietly, truthfully said,
"Memorial Day isn't special for me,
From some memories I'll never be free."

Whoever it was, those words rang true:
Back through time, out of the blue,
Sometimes unbidden recollection stirs
And another old memory slowly recurs.

A picture, an aroma, a snatch of song
Bring back the scenes, clear and strong:
A mother's smile, a lover's touch,
The faithful friend who meant so much,

The brother, always relied upon,
Whose passing was like the death of the sun;
A few acid-etched memories from the war
Constantly hover near my mind's door.

Memories, all stored in my very own way,
That have no need for a special day.
~~~

Rueful Memories:
(A City Boy Remembers Montana)
Glacier National Park

Children fishing a wooded stream
Bring back memories, like a dream
Of peace - the peace that I once knew
Before the sadness came and grew.

Trying to describe a tranquil mood,
Folks often write of 'silent woods',
Of stately trees, tall and lush
Cloaked in a calm, cathedral hush.

But it wasn't 'silence' that I heard
Not me - I listened to the birds
The music of water rushing by,
And gentle breezes like a sigh.

I heard the crickets' strident calls,
Reveled in peace, held in thrall,
Cares soothed by those idyllic woods,
I should have lingered, while I could

Beside that melodic forest brook.
I should have done what it took
To stay much longer near its banks,
Exploring down its tree-lined flanks.

Instead, I left and lived a war...
And lost my peace forevermore...
All the brooks that dance to sea
Will never bring it back to me.

Darfur

The Darfur people bleed and die,
Butchered beneath indifferent skies,
Victims of the murderous Janjaweed,
And the world pays little heed.

Congress rose in righteous wrath,
But not because of this blood bath;
Its indignation was reserved instead
For a woman many years brain-dead.

Forlorn children driven from home -
Parents slaughtered - starve alone,
Huddled up in fetal curls...
All but ignored by a blasé world

That clucks and tsks at genocide -
Then turns away while thousands die.
One hundred eighty thousand to date
Found ethnic cleansing as their fate.

A million and more are refugees,
Brutalized and forced to flee
Across the borders of Sudan
To tenuous safety in neighboring lands.

We avert our eyes from the sight,
Soberly debating their cruel plight
While across Darfur death still stalks
As we talk, and talk, and talk...and talk.
~~~

A Touch of PTSD

 Freshly forgotten, always remembered;
ancient ephemeron plucked from life
before that life had barely begun.
Evanescent and yet eternal, it lingers
in the subconscious like the irksome
ghost of a familiar song half sung.
A solid shadow that is gone at the turn
of a head; a presence as fleeting as a
brief, gentle breeze and as substantive as
the Alps. Not living, yet vitally incarnate.

A noiseless sound, an odorless aroma,
tangible scenes painted with the mind's
brush on the gauzy canvas of a dream.
A bloodcurdling, cheerful, silent scream.
Emotionless weeping, mourning laughter
reverberating in an infinite void. Proud,
unrepentant supplicants aching with joyous
remorse, supine and arrogantly begging
for forgiveness. Beyond understanding.
~~~

Life's Attrition

Another friend has gone,
and I sigh a bit more.
I can't help but feel just
a little vulnerable, a
bit achy and heart sore.

Youth's immortality, too,
is gone - victim of a long
ago war...swallowed up
by jungle paths and drowned
in rice paddies.

Echoes of indelible friendships
sound down the years. I
wonder, should I indulge
myself the dubious comfort
of a few tears?

Is it possible that one day,
all I've have left are the
memories of those eternal
ties for comfort? Will I
be the last?

Lord knows I never wanted
to be part of a war tontine.
No, no last toasts for me...
I will keep them here, safe
within, for eternity.

Occision

Folks may think the act of occision
Can be done with nonchalant precision,
Not realizing the frights
That may permeate their nights
As the result of this fateful decision.

It's a definite fact, to be sure,
That it's very difficult to inure
The mind to the strain
Of ignoring the pain
It inevitably must endure.

Some march off cheerily to war,
Revved up and totally cocksure;
But they'll eventually discover
Mars is a most demanding lover
Who'll suck them dry to the core.

So they learn as years slip on by,
While suffering the ghostly cries
Echoing through dreams
Punctuated by screams
From friends as their turns come to die.

Occision: a rare word for kill
(You can fancy it up as you will)
But after the perorations
Of politicians' orations
Who always winds up with the bill?
~~~

Hands on Treatment

The Thais are lovely people, aren't they? I walked into the BX on Don Muang Royal Thai Air Force Base one bright, sunny day wearing an elaborately embroidered shirt I'd had made in the Philippines. The clerk at the checkout counter was so taken with the shirt that she innocently began running her hands over the patterns...and unintentionally feeling me up in the process. I have to admit that I wasn't quite sure what to do, so I just stood there smiling until she finished.

Come to think of it, when I arrived on Trang-Sup in Vietnam, a bunch of the women in camp were struck by my shiny new cotton/polyester fatigues, and did pretty much the same thing to me that the Thai girl later did, except that they felt me all over, and patted my face and hands, to boot. I have never, before or since, been so thoroughly groped by strangers - at least, not without being expected to pay for it. I asked one of the American troops if the Vietnamese always greeted newcomers that way. He shook his head and said, "First time I ever saw it." Guess I'm just lucky.

Such casual intimacy took a little getting used to; Americans have got to be some of the most prudish people in the world in some ways, if not THE most strait-laced. While I realized that none of those people were remotely aware that they were 'invading my personal space' by touching me in what they considered to be a friendly and non-threatening manner, I was still a little fazed by it.

In yet another such incident at Trang-Sup, I contracted some sort of nasty skin infection that caused my face to swell to the point where my skin cracked and began to ooze an amber serum. The SF medic figured that I had gotten the infection from a barber who'd recently visited the camp.

Well, Bac Si was baffled by my steadily worsening condition and finally took me in to the Army hospital down in Tay Ninh West. The doctors there were just as stumped as the team medic, and told him to send me to Saigon. They were also interested in a scattering of black moles on my torso, saying that they were beginning to see a lot of that spreading through the troops they treated for wounds and other things. As a matter of fact, I've still got those moles. But, I digress...

When I arrived in Saigon, I checked in at the 619th Tactical Control Squadron, my parent organization. A gentleman there asked me why I needed to see a doctor. I - rather impolitely, I admit - asked him if he thought I always walked around with my face swollen and oozing plasma. He cleared his throat, looked down at my medical records, and didn't ask me any more irrelevant questions. Bureaucrats are everywhere.

I spent about a week in the hospital in Saigon; I think it was the 2nd Field Hospital. The doctor there frankly told me that he had no idea what was wrong with me, and by his own admission, was going to load his medical shotgun with a wide variety of pills and ointments - plus hourly soakings in warm compresses - and just fire it at me.

I went in on a Friday, and when the doctor came looking for me again on Monday, he didn't recognize me. He asked the medic on duty what had happened to the other guy who'd been in my bed. I assured him that I was that same guy. The doctor had wrought a miracle cure.

The swelling and lesions were completely gone, and I had even been able to shave off about two weeks' worth of scraggly beard. Doc said he was definitely writing this one up. My cure was so rapid that I felt guilty about staying in the hospital for the extra days that I was kept there to make sure the infection was gone. You would have had to see me before and after my hospital stay to really appreciate the astonishingly rapid and amazing change in my appearance.

Anyway, when I got back to camp following my miracle cure, the hootch maids once again gave me the 'hands on' treatment. When I appeared in the mess hall for my first meal after returning, they gathered 'round to check me out.

The doctor had not only succeeded in curing my skin infection, he had given me the skin of a pre-teen in the process. I didn't have so much as a pimple on my now smooth-skinned face. The women grouped around me began to murmur in awe as they gently patted and stroked my face. They even started calling me 'Babyface'.

Unfortunately, about a month after I ran out of the antibiotics and ointments the doctor had given me, my old hide slowly returned and the 'baby face' disappeared. I became my old, razor-bumpy self again, but it was nice while it lasted. I'll bet that doctor could have made a fortune if he had marketed his skin treatment. That had to be some potent stuff.

Curtis Mallory

Old Friends

I'm driving down the road toward the town of Cut
Bank, Montana (Pop. 2,000), cruising along about
seventy. My buddy, Rat, is seated beside me, riding
shotgun and weaving a fantastic fable about a
daredevil stunt bird named Charlie. Charlie is
chasing my car, doing Barrel Rolls, Immelmanns,
and other aerobatics while recklessly diving in front

of it to the warning (but delighted) shrieks and cries of his feathered buddies. They're watching this whole improbable event with horrified titillation from a safe distance above us.

I'm laughing so hard at Rat's imaginative fabrications that I'm in serious jeopardy of having an accident myself. Finally, to frantically chirped cries of, "Pull up, Charlie! For God's sake, Pull Up!" the inevitable happens. An emboldened Charlie dives too close to my hurtling grill. There's a muted "Thump!" and poor Charlie goes the way of the dinosaur; he's performed his last avian stunt. So much for showoffs. All this came about because a bird actually did fly in front of my speeding car while Rat and I were driving the long, empty forty-four miles from the radar site to the little town of Cut Bank. Rat's fertile imagination immediately kicked in and he was off and running on all cylinders...

I slowly come back to myself; it's 1966. Instead of sitting behind the wheel of my brand new '63 Ford Galaxy 500, cruising down a lonely Montana highway, I'm perched on some sandbags. I'm looking out toward a horizon where flashes of light in the muggy night sky give mute evidence of a distant firefight. This is accompanied by the far-off, almost subliminal rumble of continuous explosions. (When that rumble finally paused during the Christmas Cease Fire, its absence was a little eerie.) I've been 'watching the war'. Cut Bank's way on the other side of the world. There's a different Charlie performing tonight, and Rat isn't around to make light of his activities.

This time the guy seated beside me is named Larry - Richard "Larry" Moore - not Rat. But in his own way, he's just as talented as Curtis "Rat" Mallory. Larry plays the guitar and sings, and he's pretty good at both. Larry and I would sometimes sit for what seemed like hours on the sandbags protecting a mortar pit near the radar shack on Trang Sup. We talked idly about everything and nothing.

Sometimes, we just sat there in companionable silence. Rat had made the isolation of the remote Montana radar site bearable. Larry was now doing the same thing for me here in Vietnam. It's impossible to gauge the worth of such friendships.

Well, back to the present: It's been many years since I saw either man, right around forty for Larry, a year or so longer for Curtis, but I have never forgotten them. Each, in his own way, touched my life at a time when a friend was very much needed, whether I admitted it or not. They made me smile when times were not the brightest, and when they went on their ways out of my life, they took a little bit of the light with them.

Curtis made me laugh at times when I truly felt like killing some really shoddy people. I hasten to add this had nothing to do with Montana itself. Assholes are everywhere, and the people I speak of weren't even from Montana. Larry set my heart at ease at a time when somebody had it in mind to kill me. Totally different people with different personalities and outlooks on life; but they were just what I needed at the time I met them. Curtis was Air Force, a telephone/teletype repairman who was gifted with a Richard Pryor-like, ribald wit. Larry was an Army Green Beret and a talented musician. They were not much alike: I mostly listened while Curtis held forth; with Larry, I did a lot of the talking.

I never told them so, but I am forever grateful that God saw fit to allow them to intersect my life at those different times for the brief months that we were together. I hope they both knew that I loved them, though I doubt if I ever showed them much evidence of it. I hope they got as much out of our friendships as I did. I suspect that they did not, as I am rather reserved and they were both outgoing. I wish I could tell them now how grateful I am for having had the opportunity to know them. I miss them both.

The Real Deal

In Nam, one would think that Death came without affectation or pretense of any kind. However, he sometimes donned a smiling child's face before he wrapped his victims in his lethal embrace.

Other times, he'd hide with poisoned fangs, coiled in a narrow underground tunnel, or bury himself in the ground behind a mossy log. He would also burrow down into rice paddy dikes, waiting to explode the life from any unlucky grunt who stepped on him.

He was fond of lying in wait for the unwary soul beneath a booby-trapped wounded or lifeless body. Death hiding within death. Then again, he might greet you face to face, with a knife and a snarl.

Death rarely came peacefully, and more often than not, he stank – of rancid clothes and gamy bodies, not to mention the spilled contents of those bodies. And what are soldier-boys made of? Hearts and minds and bones and blood and guts...as well as buddies' love

Most of the time, though, Death came matter-of-factly, with a bullet or a grenade. That's not to say that his arrival was anywhere near unemotional or cut and dried. In another setting, some of these same youths would weep unashamedly because their school team had lost what was considered to be a crucial ball game.

Just how unemotional can a young man be when he's still in his teens, or barely out of them - especially when he regularly watches his friends die in in the midst of violence?

There was always emotional turmoil, accompanied by pain, noxious odors, nasty sights, and some really heartfelt, hot, bitter tears. Often it was dulled by weariness; however, it was always there, just beneath the fatigue.

But ultimately, there is only one ending - when you're dead, you're dead; not a lot of ambiguity or artificiality about that.

~~~

Old Midnight (For Cal)

Late at night, when you should be sleeping - that's when the mind starts its trip back down the years. That's when memories come unbidden and feelings that've been kept hidden away all through the day rise to hold sway. "Old Midnight" - those ancient regrets and recriminations rolled up in sorrow and pain – loves these midnight hours. He perches on the foot of the bed and lights up a smoke, settling in for the night with a smug, comfortable familiarity.

It doesn't do much good to turn on the TV as a sort of bulwark, he just keeps giving you these subliminal nudges in the ribs and before you know it you've drifted off to the stuff he's been saving up for just these hours. Bastard. You close your eyes, only to find he's brought other eyes to stare back at you, filled with those same old questions you still can't answer.

"Memories always start 'round midnight
'Round midnight
Haven't got the heart to stand those memories
When my heart is still with you
And old midnight knows it too"*

Those are the words to a love song, but Lord, how they fit these late night sessions, 'cause the heart is years and miles away from where you now lie in a futile effort to sleep, and Old Midnight definitely knows it. The 'wilderness of war' may be long in your past, but Old Midnight keeps dragging it into the present. And he doesn't care how much it hurts.

Inspired by Lou Klaiber's *Their Eyes*
*'Round Midnight - Bernie Hanighen, Cootie Williams, Thelonious Monk

Generations

In these days of strife and sorrow,
A veteran broods over tomorrow
As he remembers battles past
And regrets his were not the last,

For now his kids have gone away
Caught up in this current fray,
And his heart is filled with dread
That they'll be among the dead

Who animate his nightly dreams,
With recreations of fearsome scenes
He had prayed would dim and fade;
Instead, he's getting a new upgrade.

So the innocent continue to die
As their leaders connive and lie
In their lust for power and wealth,
Totally immersed, as usual, in self.

People can be such trusting sheep,
Expecting elected shepherds to keep
The flock safe from lupine harm,
Blithely refusing to heed the alarms.

And they're always so surprised
When, with sadly opened eyes,
They discover they've been ill-used;
There they are: betrayed and abused.

So, as generations come and go,
Exploitation continues to flow
'Round about our naïve pates;
'Manipulated' seems to be our fate.
~~~

A Sense of Loss

We look back down the misty years,
Live once more those long gone days,
Probing, examining, breathing life
Into memories through the haze.

The ache of favors not performed,
The regret for praise left unsaid,
And kindnesses we wish we'd done
For those now long among the dead.

It wasn't due to indifferent neglect
We had no way to foresee events,
We aren't gifted with clairvoyance,
So why should we now sit and lament?

We didn't fire the fatal bullet
Plan the ambush or hurl the grenade,
The war, itself, was not of our making;
That decision was by others made.

The religions in which we all believe
Tell us that the deceased are free,
No longer encumbered by the cares
That still beset you and me.

So why do we mourn their passing,
Why do we feel such lasting grief,
When we should be happily rejoicing
At the advent of their final relief?

Do we miss the familiar voices,
The friendly touch we no longer feel?
Even our companionable silences
Held an affinity that was truly real.

All these sighs and lamentations
As we sit here sad and forlorn;
Disguise a truth we may not admit:
That it's really for ourselves we mourn.

~~~

Rainbow's End

The rainbow that I search for
has no pot of gold at the end;
the final treasure that I seek
is a reunion with old friends.

The ones who heard Death's
sibilant voice whispering in their ears
signaling an end forever to
the war's insistent fears.

The ones who crouched beside me
as the mortars thundered loud,
or rushed to the aid of another
and their own waiting shrouds.

The ones who reveled with me
through the vibrant Spanish nights
on the sensual Costa Brava
in the days before firefights.

The guitars singing softly then
spoke of love and not of war;
their voices whispering to me,
"¿Quisiera bailar, mí amor?"

"¡Sí, sí, a mí, me gusta!"
and we danced away the hours,
all unaware of the coming of
the deadly monsoon showers.

The years have grown long since
Sweet Barcelona and III Corps;
but the guitars and the mortars
both sing to me once more.

Is it odd my strongest dreams
are of friends from Spanish shores
and the buddies with whom I served
in that lousy, stinking war?

Well, the friends waiting now
traveled down dissimilar streets,
but the reunion drawing closer
needs them all to be complete.

Life is Joy; Life is Sorrow:
Follow the Rainbow into Tomorrow.
~~~

With Apologies to Otis...
Diuturnity

Been searchin' all my life,
what seems like forever...
huntin' me up a bay and a dock
to sit on while I watch the tide
roll away just like the man
sang about in that sad old song.

Got the time to waste now, got
the desire to sit and waste it;
jus' ain't found that dock, yet.
Come to think of it, ain't found
the bay, neither.

Soon's I find that dock, and
soon's I spot that old bay just
spreadin' out in front of it
like it's movin' on, quiet and
easy, rollin' on towards eternity;
I'm gonna lean back and sorta
Scrunch around a bit 'til I'm real
comfy.

Then I'll break me out a bottle,
and do a little serious sittin',
sippin', and contemplatin' 'bout
stuff...and high falutin' words like
diuturnity, and if any of it's really
worth the thinkin' about....

Maybe it all jus' don't mean nuthin'.

Compassion Begins...and Ends

He slowly approaches his fallen foe
As tension fills the air,
And he warily scrutinizes
The crumpled figure lying there.

He remembers stern warnings
About booby traps he's received,
But he's young and inexperienced
And he doesn't quite believe...

The other man is still breathing,
He can see the chest fall and rise;
His own breath stops in his throat
And sweat stings his eyes.

He sees the blood staining the ground
And hears a soft, pained moan;
Compassion wills him to aid this kid
As though he were one of his own.

His rifle wavers and then lowers
As pity conquers his fear,
Then the enemy's eyes open wide...
And they are cold and clear.

The GI's rifle swings back up
As he whispers for his mother,
Realizing the mistake he's made
And that he'll never make another.

~~~

Set Me Free

Lying here in pain and fear,
I hear the cautious steps grow near;
Half-blinded by the blood in my eyes,
I see a rifle muzzle rise.

Unable to speak, barely able to hear,
I gaze into eyes filled with fear,
And somehow, I'm not a bit surprised
To also see the hate in those eyes.

You killed my family, destroyed my home,
And now I lie here dying alone;
You claim you came to set me free,
Instead you've become the death of me.

You're angry because I've killed and maimed;
If our roles were reversed, you'd do the same...
So pull the trigger and let me be,
Then carry on setting my country free.
~~~

Why Me, Indeed?

"Why me and not him? Why did I survive?
How is it he's gone, and I'm still alive?"
Perhaps the answer, unadorned, but true,
Rests in what we may inspire others to do.

We can't see ourselves through other's eyes
The value of our existence possibly lies
In our being in just the right place one day
To encourage another on his uncertain way

To climb to heights he wouldn't otherwise achieve -
To give another the strength to believe
In his own innate worth, to go on his way
To provide the answers for what we all pray.

The irony of it all is that we may never know
How, in just being, we've helped others to grow.
~~~

Thoughts in the Night
(In the Spirit of Caliber)

Just
a little reverie, a
brief return to days
gone by.

For some reason,
a dimly
remembered
face
comes back
through
the hazy years.

A
young
Green Beret
grew tired of
hanging around
camp
playing Liar's
Dice with us
'Zoomies'.

He volunteered
to
go on
patrol,
just to
"earn his pay."

Later,
they
identified
his
body
by some
of the things
he'd carried.

The misty face
I see is still smiling,
just as it was

when he strolled
jauntily away
toward
Cambodia

and his

last

payday.

Woody
2004

An attempt to imitate the writing
style of poet Lou J. Klaiber (Caliber).
~~~

Broken Bond

You spoke to me of Brotherhood;
Told me how much you cared,
Explained to me the eternal bond
That we, in fraternity, shared,

Soothed my ears with earnest words
That sang golden on the air;
But when in need I turned to you
Alas, you were not there.

It seems that your 'Brothers'
Must always agree with you
For only the things you believe,
Like the Holy Grail, are true.

All unaware, dissenting words
Slipped from my lips one day,
And, in an instant I discovered
Brotherhood had melted away.

Gone, as if it had never been,
Not a trace of it to be found,
And I was left bewildered,
Searching for the tie that "bound

Us forever" in fraternal links
You'd declared strong as steel,
Only to realize that in anger
You'd easily broken the seal.

So, go your way, my erstwhile friend,
But closely heed what you say;
I think, in the end, you'll discover
It's only yourself you've betrayed.

Written for a disappointed friend who is still
in search of either El Dorado or a Vietnam
Veterans' discussion list that actually concerns
itself solely with Vietnam Veterans... whichever
comes first.
~~~

Vinculum – Bonding

We could discuss this for days. Vinculum – what an
interesting word. Does a mother feel a stronger bond
to the child she knows she will eventually send off to
pursue his or her own individual existence or to the
husband with whom she intends to share the rest of
her life? To me, the answer would be that it varies
depending on which she perceives as needing her
the most at any given time.

There are bonds of the heart between a man and a
woman, bonds of brotherhood between friends,
bonds of familial love, and bonds of commonality
between members of a group who may not even
know one another all that well, if at all. Some are
bound to one another by similar strong, emotional
experiences, as Henry V had with his 'Band of
Brothers'.

America's Vietnam War veterans share a bond with America's veterans of World War II, the Korean, and the Mid East Wars, for instance. However, it's not the same bond that we share with those who know what 'Dinky Dow' (*Dien Cai Dau*) means. The horrors of war were and are the same, death as capricious and as imminent. Blood flows and enemies are killed at any hour of the day in all wars. Friends die, are wounded, or survive the war physically unscathed, but they still bear the invisible wounds of war within. There are bonds within bonds.
Vietnamese for 'crazy'.

We, as war veterans, all share the common bond of having participated in one of the most visceral and permanently affecting human experiences of all. But we also share the closer bond with our peers of having participated in our own individual wars. I can watch a Korean War documentary, or watch our troops battling down a street in Iraq on TV, and empathize with the participants. There are jungles in Somalia, as there are in Vietnam. However, I *lived* Vietnam; I can still smell it. My bond to Vietnam veterans is different.

And of course, the connection is not all-inclusive and unquestioning – its strength varies among members of groups or service branches. The grunts are closer to other grunts than they are to so-called 'REMFs' or to pilots, for instance. There are grunts who are 'legs' and grunts who wear parachute wings. I believe there was only one organized mass parachute jump during the Vietnam War. Still, the distinction between those who wore the paratrooper's wings and the 'legs' who didn't persisted.

The shared experiences within the larger experience of the war itself are different, so the bonds are different between the groups. It goes all the way down to individuals; we all have friends in common, but there is one friend towards whom we all gravitate. Our relationship to him is strongest of all those in the group.

I spent a year on an Army Special Forces camp. There was a strong sense of unity among the Americans in the camp, but there were understandably different ties between the Air Force radar technicians and the Army Green Berets. We were in the same camp engaged in fighting the same enemy, but we had markedly different jobs and responsibilities. Naturally, our common tie was to defend the camp during enemy attacks, stay alive, and help each other do the same.

Namvets do not blindly accept all other Namvets as unquestioningly as one is led to believe or as unequivocally as did those warriors who celebrated on Saint Crispin's Day. I will simply mention, by way of example and without elaboration, the conflict between Democrat Senator John Kerry and the Republican 'Swift Boat Veterans for Peace' who bitterly opposed his bid for the Presidency of the United States.

There are bonds that are as enduring as the universe, and bonds as tenuous and ephemeral as smoke on the wind. There are those with whom I have been united all my life, and those with whom I bonded as a matter of convenience or temporary pleasure. There are those with whom I found myself instantly and permanently connected upon our first meeting, and will never forsake, and there are those who were all but forgotten as soon as we parted.

But then, I am only human...and, until now, I had never heard the word 'vinculum' used in the sense of 'that which unites or binds'.

"...We few, we happy few, we band of brothers;
For he to-day that sheds his blood with me
Shall be my brother; be he ne'er so vile,
This day shall gentle his condition:
And gentlemen in England now a-bed
Shall think themselves accursed they were not here,

And hold their manhoods cheap whiles any speaks
That fought with us upon Saint Crispin's day."
--from Henry V by William Shakespeare
~~~

Heroes and Hollow Words of Praise

Driving slowly around Haines Point in Washington's Potomac Park, I see laughing children playing beneath warming skies. Older folks jog, cycle, or walk along, getting in their daily exercise, some accompanied by the music from their tiny portable jukeboxes. Out on the Potomac, Georgetown's rowing teams practice, their oars flashing in and out of the water in unison as they scull along to their cox'n's chant.

I roll on past 'The Awakening', a giant man emerging from the earth with his mouth stretched wide in a silent yell (or scream). Some years back, a lady lost control of her car and did some serious damage to the poor fellow's head. This has since been repaired, and he appears none the worse for the injury.

If I continue along this road, I will eventually pass the Roosevelt Memorial and approach the Lincoln Memorial, which looks down the National Mall past the Viet Nam Wall and the Korean War Memorial to the World War II Memorial at the far end of the Reflecting Pool. Tributes to the honored dead of three wars are gathered here.

I suppose that soon, there will be a fourth memorial, one to honor those who have died, and are yet dying, in the Middle East wars. But now, unlike these other revered dead, the bodies of fallen soldiers from Iraq and Afghanistan are being smuggled home in secret as though they had committed some heinous act. Their return can't be photographed or televised; a curtain of secrecy has been drawn between them and the nation.

So many of us Viet Nam veterans still complain bitterly about the reception – or lack of a reception – we got as we straggled home from our war. Except for family and friends, we were variously spat at, scorned, or met with total indifference, depending upon who's doing the telling. Yet we seem not to care about the treatment accorded the bodies of the service people returned from the Mideast conflict.

The nation goes on and on about supporting our troops and standing up for America, but it virtually ignores this implicit insult. The prevailing opinion is, of course, that these Flag-draped coffins are hidden from public view so as not to give graphic evidence of the loss of American lives that might help fuel protest against a war gradually increasing in unpopularity.

Whatever the reason, I think it's indecent that our fallen sons and daughters should be smuggled home so ignominiously - in the back door, so to speak - as though they are unseemly objects that need to be hidden away and disposed of as soon as possible. It reflects badly on America.

~~~

A Troubling Taciturnity

Of what would you have me speak,
What would you have me say?
Are you interested in my thoughts
Or just intrigued by the way

I sometimes sit in silence,
My veiled eyes fixed within
As I look back on horrific scenes
From places I have been?

Do you really care why I brood?
Would you like to share this mood?
Do you truly want to come with me...
Live these things I can't help but see?

They've dwelt within me for so long
In the private places of my soul
They're now an integral part of me
And cannot be so easily told

To someone who cannot imagine
How such terrible things came to be
Though I long to purge myself of them
So I can once again be free.

I beg you, have a little patience,
And wait for just a bit more
Until the day I can come to you
To share what makes my heart sore.

Please...never, never, ever think
These are secrets I wish to keep;
If I could, I'd give them all away
In exchange for dreamless sleep.

But, for now, and just a while longer
...Hopefully, not for eternity,
With your patient understanding
I'll keep it all inside of me.
~~~

No Regrets

There's always regret for things not done,
A little heartache for songs left unsung.
Not that my voice is all that great,
It's just that it seems a part of my fate
 That I would never climb all those hills
I occasionally glimpse beckoning me still...
A bit of yearning for what might have been
Had I not tarried so long in the glens.

Yet it was worth those moments of bliss,
The sweet desire, that lingering kiss
That held me enthralled in love's embrace,
A willing captive, away from the chase.

But, of course, I could not forever stay,
And after awhile, I'd go on my way,
Still in search of that magical thing…
Adventure, or Fame, or Eternal Spring.

So I chased my gossamer youth along
With blood pulsing, vibrant and strong,
And never a thought that alas, one day
The pulse would slow and my hair turn gray
Before I accomplished all I had in mind,
And I'd have to leave the chase behind.

But glimmering rainbows will always be there
With crystal songs faintly heard on the air,
Calling to me softly when I start to fret,
Gentle reminders that I have little to regret.
~~~

Swift Sorrow

Pain renewed,
Memories strewed
Coming unglued
From the pain
What was gained
By a 'Band of Brothers'
Belittling each other?
The bond is unglued
Everybody's screwed.
Dumb-ass feud
~~~

Loyalty

Loyalty…a bond, a belonging,
An unyielding, impenetrable tie
That binds us together forever -
A link between you and I.

A mutual understanding
That cements us together as one,
A coming together of interests
That should last 'til life is done.

But, the path of blind fidelity -
Is it the best route to follow?
For your lyrical, inspiring words
May be self-serving and hollow,

Concealing your selfish agenda
While allaying my suspicions
Of what your true motivation is
As you lead me on to perdition.

Fealty and faithfulness, blind
Allegiance and well-nurtured hope
Can lead the naive believer
Over the edge of a slippery slope.

Faith is much too precious a gift
To be so easily tendered,
Offered to the facile-tongued,
Greedy for such surrender.

Distasteful as it may be to some,
Loyalty must be guardedly offered,
Not given from a sense of duty
Or otherwise easily proffered,

Lest we come to realize one day,
As we waken with a sickening shock,
That we'd been helping out the wolf
As he gathered in our flock.
~~~

Among the Monuments

Standing at the Lincoln Memorial,
gazing down the National Mall
one thinks of these memorials,
 WW II to the Viet Nam Wall...

The many souls they commemorate,
the sacrifices of them all...
Boys and girls turned women and men
answering Liberty's call.

And the living people gathered,
in summer's heat or chilly autumn rain;
some come to leave a token of love,
others come to ease their pain,

or lift a burden of long held guilt,
heavy as if it were truly earned.
Acknowledging bonds forged in pain...
and truths forever learned.

Veteran and civilian alike,
they have come here seeking release;
hoping to find among graven stones
a measure of lasting peace.
~~~

Safe Harbor
PTSD

Proudly, I embarked on life's seas,
But today I am shocked to find
There, between the world and me,
The barrier reefs of my mind.

So, here I am, full of longing,
Gazing out upon beckoning seas,
Aching to depart, my soul on fire...
But locked in a prison that is me.

 When did I arrive in this harbor?
Why did the reefs slowly form?
At first, I was buoyed by their presence;
They protected me from the storms.

Now, as I drift slowly backward
Til my keel gently grounds on the sand,
I fear I will remain here forever,
Marooned on this sheltered strand.

The sails have all been lowered,
And the waves idly lap at my hull
While a tear slowly wells and spills over
for a life grown barren and dull.

©5/10/2004 Thurman P. Woodfork
(With an assist from Nancy L. Meek)
 ~For all those bunker-bound souls~
~~~

Fame

What the hell does a GI know about fame?
How does that figure in with his game
Of ducking the brass and scamming Old Sarge
While narrowly avoiding being hit with a charge
Of 'Failure to Repair' for that extra time
Spent shacked up in town instead of on the line?

He might be famous for drinking more booze
Than anybody ever while on a Med cruise
Or for the fastest time in the Barefoot Dash
When he discovered that 'lady' demanding cash
Was a Billy Boy built to the exact same specs
As any male who ever swabbed a deck.

Or, maybe the reason for his great renown
Is the time he won the undisputed crown
As the best trader with the smoothest rap
When he managed to con an unsuspecting chap
Into supplying all the fixings for a squadron spree
For four hundred bucks in recalled MPC.

It's an elusive thing, this whimsical fame
And your average GI's not looking for acclaim
He's more concerned with managing his day
In order to keep well out of the way
Of Chiefs and Tops and Gunnies and the rest.
A day free of them is an unqualified success.
~~~

Hearts and Minds

A Marine, some shoes, a child in need
The deliberate planting of a seed
That must grow into a sturdy tree
Of trust before these people are free.

Force by itself will not win the war;
Conquering leaves a suppurating sore
That festers behind subjugated eyes
Eventually erupting as emotions rise.

"Hearts and Minds" may well sound trite
But must be employed along with might.
The rock hard fist in a mailed glove
Can never engender the kind of love

That will allow our troops to leave in peace
And give our soldiers their deserved release
So they can come home and put down their guns
Knowing their job is over - and well done.
'Til next time.
~~~

High Steppin' John

When High Steppin' John went home today
We old friends solemnly gathered to pray
And remember the times we'd spent together
In many different places, and in all kinds of weather

But soon the sadness gave way to smiles
As we recalled the lighthearted miles
Our feet danced over as the years eased by:
There really was no need to cry.

For High Steppin' John wasn't called that by chance
His time on earth held joy and romance;
His easy nature transcended the mundane
Which is how he came to be tagged with that name.

He could out-drink any man, and out-work him, too
And he'd sing you a little song when things got blue,
For mopin' and bitchin' weren't part of his game
And the people he befriended soon felt the same.

Yep, High Steppin' John went home today
With many a warm thought to bless his way
Though the light, just now, may seem a tad dim,
It shone brighter for years because of him.

So ladies and gents, good friends gathered here,
Let's remember him as he lived, and be of good
cheer
We've sent him on his way, now step up for a beer
And we'll toast old John with eyes free of tears.

For all the good friends who've gone on.
~~~

"Friendly Fire" Ain't

While viewing the photos designed to inspire pity
For victims in Fallujah and those other Iraqi cities
Where people were mangled in the jaws of war
I wondered what else the photographers saw?

Who, I wondered, actually hurled the first grenades
Or fired the first shots that began the cannonades
Which ended in the firefights, that now raise such
ire?
Could the injured be the victims of their own
'Friendly Fire'?
~~~

Trang Sup Memories

One minute I was sound asleep, the next I was wide-awake, pop-eyed with alertness, straining to pierce the inky darkness. Then I heard it again, the sound that had awakened me, a chilling, sibilant whisper, "You die, GI; you die." It came to me with a little electric thrill of shock: the bastard was in my hooch room! I realized that I was holding my .45 in my hand, on full cock. It always hung from the mosquito-netting frame right over my head while I slept, but I didn't remember taking it from the holster. I didn't even remember moving, other than to open my eyes.

I lay still, waiting for some sound of movement, and finally, the voice whispered again, sounding almost gleeful, "You die, GI." I realized he was not in the room with me but outside my window, talking through the locked shutters, and he couldn't see me any more than I could see him. Suddenly, I was completely furious and I slipped out of the cot, forgetting for once about the deadly kraits and cobras that lurked beneath my bunk every night, waiting for just such an opportunity.

I was intent on scaring this turkey as thoroughly as he'd frightened me. I slept fully dressed, so I only had to slip into my boots and sneak the M-16 off the wall. So far, I hadn't made a sound; the cot had not creaked as I slid out of it. I inched the cubicle door open and tiptoed down the hall, feeling my way in the darkness. It took a moment to find the key to unlock the door, and then I was outside; still, I thought, without making a sound other then cocking the .45 when I first awakened.

I could see the Sergeant of the Guard sitting by his radio in the Team House, but he wasn't looking in my direction. Sam, the monkey mascot, was awake and stared at me owlishly through the mesh of his cage as I snuck to the edge of the barracks and peeked around the corner. Nobody was near my window or any of the others. The building was white, so I would have seen anyone close to it even in the darkness. There were the usual CIDG guards on the wall; some were sitting on the sandbags around the mortar emplacement a little distance from my window.

Not a soul knew what I was talking about, even the ones who could speak enough English to understand what I was saying. They all swore that they had seen nobody near the window nor heard anybody say anything. Nobody got close to me, and they all sort of managed to keep from getting directly in front of me as though they were afraid I would shift the rifle from semi-port to bear on them if they did. I finally gave up and went back to the barracks.

As I started to enter the building, it suddenly occurred to me to wonder if maybe this hadn't been somebody's warped idea of a joke. There certainly were Viet Cong agents and sympathizers inside the camp. Suppose some of them had been trying to lure me into doing just what I had done; come alone around the barracks in the pitch-black night to where they waited. "You die, GI," could have turned out to be a fatal reality and not a joke at all. I got a little shivery again.

I unlocked the barracks, went in and locked the door behind me, then felt my way back down the hall to my cube, and hung the rifle back on the wall. This time I turned the light on and examined my cot and the space beneath it for cobras, kraits, and other deadly reptiles before turning off the light and crawling under the mosquito netting, making sure it was securely tucked in all the way around.

I put the .45's hammer on half-cock and returned the gun to its holster. I closed my eyes, half expecting to hear that sly, amused, whispered voice again, but nothing broke the silence except the far off, almost subliminal thud of the omnipresent bombardments. Eventually, I drifted off to sleep and awoke later on in time for duty, having survived bad judgment once again. Whoever had paid me that nocturnal visit never returned to my window again, although I heard that he whispered in others. Guess he just liked waking people up.

~~~

Where Is the Warrior King?

When we hear men speak of bravery and brotherhood in war and we watch them as they kneel in prayer over the limp, still warm form of a slain friend, we should do more than empathize or parrot self-righteous prattle about 'supporting the troops'.

When we see them rocking in bone-deep anguish, clasping close in helpless grief the bloody remains of what was once a living, vibrant person, perhaps we should demand to know, "Where is our 'Warrior King'?"

Maybe he should be there on the field of battle with his soldiers.

Let him inhale the awful odors of violent death; let him hear the cries and moans of the injured, let him live with the open wounds and the bloody body parts strewn about by the careless hand of war while rockets are still exploding and bullets still ricocheting.

Let the genesis of future nightmares and vivid flashbacks be planted deep to germinate and finally bloom in his psyche.

As it is now, few of our leaders have experienced at first hand the true, gut-wrenching, elemental emotions and feel of war. Some say that's not necessary; I say, it can't hurt.

Soldiers fight over the same streets and neighborhoods again and again, and they do it because men thousands of miles from the actual fighting and dying mandated unsuccessful, shortsighted strategies. Would the orders have been different if the leaders were sharing the battlefield dangers with the soldiers?

Patton said that he did not want to die for his country; he wanted to insure that the enemy died for his. I echo that and would add: But first, make sure that it's necessary for anyone at all to die.

Actually, we really don't need a 'Warrior King'; we do need more competent civilian leaders who will listen to and rely upon the judgment of the military leaders who have to implement their orders.

I'm afraid we don't have the equivalent of a 'Warrior King' or leaders who will wisely use the admirals and generals who stand in his place.

If we did, perhaps our efforts in this 'War on Terror' would have been concentrated more in Afghanistan in pursuit of bin Laden and his terrorists. If we did, perhaps less time would be spent vacationing down on the ranch while our youth bleed and die in the sands and streets of the Middle East. Just speculating.

Different Drums

I suppose one must suffer the cranky twit
Who never seems to quite get it:
While contrarily marching to his own drumbeat,
He is quite apt to get trampled by the feet
Of all those who aren't quite so perverse.

When one insists upon violating the norm
Of traditional behavior, why he's subject to scorn
By those who follow the conventional way;
All of which, is of course to say -
When others go forward, don't shift into reverse.

What's one to do with this contrary soul?
Perhaps we can decide that he's just being droll
And silently suffer his occasional rants
While resisting the desire to flame his pants,
Which, of course, would only make matters worse.
~~~

Empty Hours

Another New Year has begun and I remain awake in
the quiet house. The TV set in the living room and
the one on the back porch are set to different
channels and, not disposed to get up, I alternately
listen to each in turn as some sound penetrates my
wandering mind and briefly calls me back to the
present.

Rod Stewart is singing "Maggie May" in the living
room while, out on the porch, the LA sheriff denies
manhandling Michael Jackson during the King of
Pop's brief stay in jail. Actually, I'm not interested in
either program, and soon return to my thoughts..

And as usual, at the stroke of midnight, a bunch of
the neighborhood nimnulls stepped outside and
began firing their guns into the air. Somebody
should ship them all off to Iraq or Afghanistan where
they could get their fill of firing weapons. As for me,

I was strangely undisturbed by the rattle of small arms fire, probably because I knew it was coming and was waiting for it.

I idly wondered what would happen if one of the celebrators got conked on the noggin by one of the bullets they were recklessly firing into the air. More than likely, the projectile would probably fall on some innocent person walking along the street instead of beaning the dummy who'd fired it.

Well, this year is almost five hours old, and this musing really isn't going anywhere, so I may as well hang it up. The living room TV is now busy hyping a 'Girls Gone Wild/Endless Spring Break' video, and I wonder how many mothers are having minor heart attacks at the sight of their daughters gyrating about the screen. If, indeed, those really are college girls. It finally intrudes enough on my reminiscing to make me hunt up the remote and change channels.

Now I'm informed that the available lotteries in the Greater Washington area have a combined total of nearly half a billion dollars. What are the chances of some lucky soul hitting both? Almost makes me wish I had bought a couple of tickets.

Well, enough of this aimless meandering in the wee hours. Sitting here at the dining room table, I've mentally visited Spain, Montana, Alaska, and Viet Nam, along with some old boyhood haunts. Could these hours I've spent rummaging through my memory really be classified as empty?

Not really, they were richly populated with the people and events of my past. I had camped out, perched on a sandbagged wall and watched a war, hiked through Glacier National Park, got a little drunk on the Ramblas in Barcelona, and dreamed awhile on white Mediterranean sands. Not to mention enjoying the magnificent view while freezing my buns off riding the tram between bottom and top sites in Tin City, Alaska.

Well, to be honest, I guess there was a little bit of regret, a tiny sense of loss that the vital, agile young man who had done these things was now just sitting quietly, gray haired, half lost in reverie, dreaming away the night hours. But, no...not empty hours, no emptiness at all.
~~~

Mind Shadow

In my younger days, I would have thought nothing of walking the distance between my house and the Pentagon. Before my dogs died, I used to walk them from my house to the Capitol. Now, after over twenty years of traveling the world in the name of freedom, it seems the menace has found its way to my own neighborhood. When I joined the Air Force nearly fifty years ago, an attack by such a faceless enemy was inconceivable.

As the bright sunlight filters in through the window, a familiar, distant thunder is heard; a jet circles in the skies over Washington. Years ago, when I was a child, planes flew directly over my house as they entered the landing patterns for National Airport or Bolling Air Force Base. They were a mild irritant because they momentarily disrupted the TV reception as they made their descent to earth.

Bolling long ago closed its runways and the flight pattern for National has been changed. But this plane isn't landing; it is circling high over the city on a patrol, guarding against possible terrorist attacks.

It's far above my house, its engines a remote mutter, yet it casts a shadow through the pattern of sunlight shining through the trees and playing upon my living room wall. It overlays the dancing leaves with an
invisible but tangible shadow of anger and fear.

Deadly explosions and sneaking attackers are things

that I thought I had left behind in another life in another country. Yet, here they are again; they have followed me home. And an old, long sublimated feeling returns, vivid as ever: an impotent, banked, helpless rage. The same anger I felt in the bunker down in Tay Ninh after I returned to Trang Sup TDY.

I was waiting for a flight out, so I had no defensive position to man. I just sat in the bunker with some others, listening to and feeling the explosions erupting overhead outside while someone else confronted the unseen enemy.

Dimly, I can hear children laughing outside as the sound of the fighter fades into the distance. Remembered sounds and odors recede; again, I'm in a room bright with sunlight instead of a darkened bunker.

The shadow dissolves back into leaves moving lazily in the random breezes. The anger is slower in receding.

~~~

Another Veterans' Day

I have seen their laughing faces,
With crinkled, smiling eyes
Changed by war to somber masks
Where now only sorrow lies.

What happened to the gung ho kids
Who left home, courage high?
Well, some came back, if alive,
With eyes that just want to cry.

How is it that some could survive
A war's most vicious wrath,
And, when at last returning home,
Find a serene and peaceful path

To follow for the rest of their days
While other comrades-in-arms
Seem to have experienced
Deep and incurable harm?

They all saw gut-wrenching sights,
Felt the blood ooze, sticky and warm,
Fought through rice paddies and jungles
And across sand dunes and farms.

They reacted alike with visceral pain
To the searing loss of friends,
They lived as one the perilous nights
And days that never seemed to end.

They flew the vengeful, fast-moving, jets
And the chopper medevacs;
They fired off rockets, dropped napalm
Or were tireless airborne FACS.

They manned the door guns and fired
the flares that ripped the dark asunder,
They soared above the smoking earth
as it throbbed to their Rolling Thunder.

They huddled in the darkened rooms,
Glued to their radar scopes,
Knowing the bright dots they guided
Were some besieged grunts' final hope.

They patrolled the base perimeters
Along with their brave canines,
They drove the trucks, cooked the
meals, and detonated mines.

They bandaged wounds and operated
to save thousands of lives;
They wept for the ones who didn't make it
And cared for the ones who'd survive.

They all were numbed by constant death,
The pain, the weariness, the terror.
Yet some somehow found inner peace,
While other lives lost their fervor.

It wasn't a simple matter of guts,
For having courage does not spare
Anyone the dreams and flashbacks
That can, unbidden, suddenly flare.

It's something that lies deep within,
The essence of who we are,
That allows some souls to heal themselves
While others remain deeply scarred.

It's something that I contemplate
As we observe another Veterans' Day;
And I wish for us all eternal peace
When we come to the end of our ways.
~~~

Closure

Once again from the embattled past,
More brothers have been returned at last,
Recovered from their forlorn beds,
To rest in honor at home instead.

So many more remain behind
Though yet alive in loving minds.
They're still lost to the yearning arms,
Of those who prayed they'd return unharmed.

Since that event is yet to be,
God grant this Nation will finally see,
On some soon, long-awaited day,
Her last 'Nam son come home to stay.

So many offered all there was to give,
And we pray that some still live.
If they do, God sustain those men...
Please, for us all, let it come to an end.

The Person Who Used To Be

What a shame no one will ever again see
That singular person who used to be:
The one who loved, and laughed, and vied...
For while still living, he turned away, and died.

There was a time he could inspire with a word,
But that strong voice will never again be heard,
Even though he has not yet ceased to speak;
His words are now unfocused and bleak.

His potential gone a-ghosting, but shunning pity,
He wanders alone through the streets of the city
Or languishes away in a dreary psychic cell,
Reliving the memories of his own private hell.

What happened, you wonder, to cause such a
change?
What was the trauma that managed to derange
All that was wonderful in this precious life,
And fill it instead with heartache and strife?

The recurring nightmares of shadowed jungle paths,
Gravid with the imminence of sudden blood baths,
And the cry of the friend, who voiced his last sound
As, calling, he spun and fell, lifeless, to the ground.

There was no refuge; even when 'safe' in the rear,
He knew that he must go back into the fear,
To the rage, death, and terror that would not abate
Until he reached that longed-for date:

The shimmering DEROS - the day he was free
To return to the person he could no longer be,
To battle strange ailments, disillusion, and sighs,
Until, still living, he turns away... and dies.
~~~

My brother and I served in Vietnam together; he arrived a month or so before I did. He was at Pleiku; I was at Trang Sup in Tay Ninh Province.

A Visit to The Wall

Some years ago, they were having a ceremony at The Wall. I asked my brother if he'd ever been to The Wall, and he said no. Knowing that, during that time in his life, he did not like to go out alone, I asked if he would visit The Wall with me, and was surprised when he said yes.

So, we went down, parked the car quite a ways back from The Wall, and walked along with other people headed for the ceremony. There was quite a crowd down by The Wall when we arrived, and my brother stopped beside the statue of The Three Soldiers. Some Big Wheel was giving a talk, and we stood there listening for a time, slightly apart from the crowd.

A TV cameraman, scanning the faces looking toward The Wall, paused for a moment with his video cam pointed at us. I suppose he was attracted by the obvious family resemblance. Two brothers, solemnly looking down at The Wall.

After a bit, he continued his scanning.

A little later, my brother said, I'm ready to go, and I replied, OK, you don't want to get any closer? He answered, Not now; The Wall will be here for a time. So we left, each with his own thoughts.
~~~

The Penitent
Survivor's Guilt

Musing with grim memories
wrapped 'round him like a cloak,
while hollow-eyed wraiths
swirl about like spectral smoke,

his mind drifts through the rubble
of his mournful recollections,
masticating those doleful days
like chewing sweet confections.

He gently strokes the aching
as though caressing a sweet lover,
yet searching, probing, scanning,
always seeking to discover

some reason for the haunting -
a cure for the psychic pain
or perhaps at least the coda
for this damned, recurring refrain

that plays forever and ever
on the soundtrack in his brain...
a funeral march, an alluring dirge,
a melodious elegy.

Caught in the mournful rhythm
of his personal threnody,
he molds a sharpened stiletto
forged of steely, unearned guilt

and thrusts it like a harpoon
into his vitals to its hilt.
Then, rising like the Phoenix
ascending from the flames,

he takes his seat and wearily
begins his penance once again.
~~~

A Night in Saigon

This particular story isn't about the times when the
barbarians were not only at the gates but in the wire
as well, with malice in their hearts. I'm reminded of a
different sort of conflict. As a matter of fact, I wasn't
on Trang-Sup at all when this took place.

The scene that plays behind my drowsing eyes is of me and the "Cambode" riding on the backs of motorcycles down a large boulevard in Saigon, probably Tu Do Street. We were both comfortably smashed, which is why I was on the motorcycle in the first place; I certainly wouldn't have gotten on one sober. Riding them must have been Cambode's idea.

Most of that night is a blur; I don't remember where we went, or what we did. I just remember heading back for home alone, still on a motorbike. It could have been the same one I started the evening riding. The operator, ignoring my protests, suddenly decided to take a short cut. I found myself traveling through an ominously dark and unsavory part of town, something I wasn't too happy about even in my cheerfully pickled state.

The driver paid little heed to my protests until I remembered, wonder of wonders, that I had neglected to check my .45 in at the 619th along with my other gear when I arrived on Tan Son Nhut from Trang- Sup. Somehow, that always seemed to happen when we came in to Saigon. As usual when I discovered my mistake, I couldn't leave the gun laying around the team house, so there it was, nestled snugly in my waistband beneath my shirt.

It was remarkable how quickly my chauffeur's cooperation improved when he felt the muzzle of that large weapon behind his ear. Or maybe it was the cheery click of it being cocked that so focused his attention. At any rate, he soon found his way back to more brightly lit, populated streets where we parted company amicably and went our separate ways.

I think we parted friends; at least, he didn't wait to be paid and didn't call me *dinky-dow until he looked back as he was speeding off and saw that both my hands were empty. I guess riding along with an angry drunk pressing a .45 in the crack of his ass had soured his disposition somewhat.

He didn't know that I had quietly lowered the hammer and slid the safety on, so a sudden bump wouldn't have instantly endowed him with a second anal orifice. I really wasn't as much worried about his health as I was about accidentally gelding myself. That .45 was snuggled against both his and my more treasured parts.

Our little adventure had sobered me up considerably. I got off that bike a lot more clear-headed than I had been when I got on it. At least, thanks to my absent-mindedness with the hand gun...and the driver's sudden grasp of English...I didn't have to strangle the little rascal and learn to operate a motorcycle myself that night. But I was just flat not about to go wherever it was that he'd planned to take me. Call me a candy-ass.

Now, I cite absent-mindedness about having the gun handy since I would never, ever have deliberately disobeyed orders and carried a loaded .45 with me onto the light-hearted, tranquil streets of downtown 1966 Saigon. Not me.
*Americanization of *Dien cai dau* - crazy.
~~~

Sweet Liberty

How much do people who have always had true liberty actually value it...well, not so much value it as appreciate what a precious gift they possess? I remember, years ago, standing at the window of my hotel room in Madrid watching a kid of about twelve or thirteen walking down the street. I could tell from his carriage more than by the cut of his clothing that he was an American.

He strode self-assuredly through the Spaniards around him – proud people themselves – as though he owned their streets. He had the arrogance of freedom, that innate confidence that comes from enjoying unfettered national liberty. He had never known anything else in his young life. Even though he was momentarily alone in a foreign country, he was an American, and special, and he knew it. He wore his nationality like an invisible suit of impenetrable armor.

But I fear those days of unquestioning belief in our national invulnerability are history; Americans can no longer blithely stride along the world's avenues, secure in their national identity, and this is leading to a domestic crisis.

There are so many of us who grew up with that special awareness of being free, of being Americans. We take our liberty for granted; so much so that we feel no special need to defend it from usurpation by fellow Americans. It is, after all, our right by birth as citizens of the United States. It has always been there for most of us.

We ingested liberty with our mothers' milk and it's difficult for us to believe that other Americans - who, on the surface, seem to espouse our own beliefs - would, for their own selfish purposes conspire to take it away from us. We do, after all, have "Constitutional Guarantees." Our attention is focused sharply outward on foreign terrorists and not inward toward domestic duplicity.

This allows us to fall under the sway of alarmists, to heed the pseudo-patriotic rhetoric from politicians who were elected to office to protect our interests. Unfortunately, they're more concerned with advancing the interests of the lobbyists and multi-national corporations that line their pockets than they are with safeguarding the rights of the electorate.

America is slowly losing its liberty even as we common folk band together to defend it. We're unmindful that most of the people who lead us have never personally lifted a hand in defense of the freedoms of this nation, or those of any individual outside their own select circle.

I stand in baffled frustration as I watch the people head obediently off to figurative shearing sheds to have their liberties clipped. They go along, baa-ing contentedly, like well-fed sheep under the deceitful direction of lupine shepherds and their servile sheepdogs. Even some of the rams...especially the rams...trot along dutifully.

Who is there to protect us from these conniving predators who have taken deception a step beyond the cunning wolf of the cautionary *fable? They've moved beyond sheep skins and now wear the shepherds' clothing. To protest their chicanery is to be seen as seditious, which in itself is a diminution of liberty. My, my, what big teeth you have, dear Guardians of the Republic's Liberty!

*Matthew 7:15 - Beware of false prophets, which come to you in sheep's clothing, but inwardly they are ravening wolves.
~~~

What Is a Soldier?

What makes someone a soldier? Well, just to take a guess, sometimes all it took was a letter from the SSS. Hell, a soldier can come from anywhere in our present society, and be male or female, wealthy or working class; makes no difference if you truly have the desire. Look at the recent examples of Patrick Miller, Shoshanna Johnson, Lori Piestewa, and Jessica Lynch, to name a few of the more well-known members of the current rank and file.

Do people really join up for those great sounding, patriotic reasons like love of country and Mom's apple pie? Do they really yearn to protect the Constitution and keep this country free? Or maybe way, way down in their secret heart of hearts, they're just adrenalin junkies. Out for the adventure, looking for a free trip around the world, exploring exotic places like Khe Sahn and Kosovo.

There is a certain amount of joie de vivre to be had in wearing a helmet and NBC uni in 100 plus degree desert heat, or freezing one's unmentionables off in a snowed-in tent on an icy mountaintop in Korea. Added zest comes from having unseen, surly people drop mortars on you or craftily pick off the last friend from your original outfit so that you can hold him in your arms as he bleeds to death waiting for a Medevac.

Of course, there are some who choose to go adventuring on the seas, regularly visiting such interesting places as Japan, Italy, The Philippines, Yankee Station, Yemen. It's said that the deck of an aircraft carrier is one of the most dangerous places in the world. That could, in itself, be adventure enough for many people. Okay, okay, so you spent most of the trips between ports down in the bowels of the ship in the engine room. So what? Think of the great camaraderie you developed down there with your hard working friends.

Then, one may simply decide to join the military for reasons as prosaic as earning money to get a college education after the enlistment is up. But what makes so many reenlist after that first tour is over, and then the second tour, and so on until they realize that they've somehow become 'The Dreaded Lifer?'

What is it, really? It can't be the great pay or excellent working conditions. Crawling through rice paddies or triple canopy jungles while attracting leeches and sniper fire can't logically be called a 'perk'. No, it's something intangible, like the enduring bonds forged with the folks who crept through that jungle or froze on that mountain with you. However, some people do their twenty without ever hearing a shot fired in anger or having spent any time on the remote, frozen tundra of some tiny, isolated spot like an Air Force arctic radar station.

Can it be that there are people who do require and enjoy the discipline and structure inherent in the military life? They need order, a sense of responsibility, the close-knit teamwork, camaraderie, and, yes, love required of an effective unit. A unit that, after all the trappings are put aside, is tasked to place its very existence on the line in the continuing defense of a nation. They are the bulls that always instinctively station themselves on the perimeter of the herd and face outward to deal with any danger that stalks their fellows.

Man, after all is said and done, is a herd animal, though we may call our particular herd a family, a squad, a neighborhood, a tribe, a city, or a nation. Perhaps, in time, the limits of our herd will be defined only by the boundaries of the universe.

But, to be perfectly honest and to stop dancing all around the question, I really don't know what makes a true soldier. Maybe some do it because Dad was a Lifer. Or, maybe like me, they just looked great in a uniform. Plus, as *Andy says, "We get to march in parades---And nobody can beat our funerals."
*Nicholas Andreacchio, Col., USA (Ret.)
~~~

Who Shares My Journey?

Who accompanies me on this long journey through life? They're legion; some have walked with me for only a day or so before slipping off to become part of yesterday's memories, while others remain who were witnesses to my first steps on this road.

They've watched me triumph and fail, helped me up when I fell, encouraged me when I tried to turn back in doubt. Others have placed obstacles in my way, jeered when I hesitated, applauded when I stumbled and rejoiced when I wandered off down some interesting side road that ultimately led to nowhere.

But someone always appeared who knew a route back to the main road and showed the way. And there was also much to be learned on those detours. Every now and then, it was I who showed someone the way back to their own route. There is a lot of joy and satisfaction in being such a guide. But always, I had to return to my own path.

Now, some tell me that I have reached a point in life's odyssey when I should ease into the rest area on the side of the road and linger there while I look back down that long, long highway and contemplate the twists and turns, the elevations and the low points.

I think not; my shoes still have sturdy soles, and a little brushing can still bring out the luster of the leather. Like Frost, I will only pause for a little while. I, too, have promises to keep, and hopefully, many more miles to go before I sleep. And there's still a song or two that I have not sung.

There is joy in life, and celebrations yet to be found. I look forward to discovering what lies around the next bend, or on the far side of that mountain there in the distance. And, of course, there's always the anticipation of meeting the folks who will appear to share this next part of my journey.

~~~

The In-Betweeners

I was neither a grunt nor an REMF, but somewhere in between. I should explain; I was an Air Force radar repairman stationed on an Army Special Forces A Team camp. That has provided me with some interesting memories. Every now and then, when I think of those long ago times, I relive the unexpressed anxiety when days slipped by and friends out on patrol didn't return on schedule.

To me the hours seemed to slow to a crawl as the time passed. Then, one morning would reveal that they had returned in the night while we slept, and the world was whole again. There was a breath of relief, silent thanks, and a weight lifted from the soul. All unexpressed, hidden in a smiling joke.

There was the nagging belief, or superstition, that a display of too much affection or friendship would somehow conjure up a jinx. Real affection was therefore not overtly displayed. It may have been foolish, but that's how I felt.

There is the enduring memory of the youngster who went on patrol when he wasn't scheduled to go because he wasn't "being paid to sit around camp playing Liar's Dice with a bunch of Zoomie Legs." He became separated from the others during an ambush, and they were unable to find him immediately.

I never saw him again, but when he was found a few days later, we were told that his body had been mutilated. He was full of good spirits when he left, so I prefer to remember him as I last saw him, smiling and happy. Lord knows he earned his pay that day.

I sometimes thought that the people back Stateside were very fortunate. We 'In-Betweeners' not only watched our friends depart from 'home,' we had a much better idea of what they were doing - and what was being done to them - while we waited for their return.

Another time, I remember the voices from the radio as a sister camp was desperately resisting being overrun, and the angry, frustrated anguish as our men, unable to assist, listened as their friends fought and died. Courageous men do weep, bitterly and unashamedly.

Curiously, I remember little of the times when we were attacked: the fiery stream of red tracers hosing down from above the flares, accompanied by a burping roar as Spooky circled invisibly overhead; helicopter gunships darting like vengeful, death-dealing fireflies; mortars exploding, machine guns and rifles rattling.

The most vivid memory is not of an attack on the camp, but of one on the village right next to us. The worst part was when it was over and we went to aid the villagers. How do you comfort a burned, bleeding child when you cannot even speak his language?

But, oddly enough, the memories of more peaceful times are much clearer. I suppose my mind prefers to recall the periods sitting on the sandbags watching the muted, dancing flashes from distant conflicts off on the horizon than replaying the episodes that were, as they say, up close and personal.

It is, I suppose, a defense mechanism. If you don't remember the more stressful times, there is less guilt felt in having survived them relatively unscathed.

~~~

That Other Place

Down through all the mourning years
Fortunately, I have come to find,
Untouched by echoes of recurring fears
This special corner in my mind

Where demons do not come to play
And plague my nights or fret my days
With memories of that bygone fray.
One day, I heard a quiet voice say:

"In this place gloom may not exist;
This is for those who did not die.
There's no need to sit and list
Comrades for whom we have to cry."

"Savor the guitar lightly strummed,
Join in the games of pickup ball
And snatches of song softly hummed;
Laze a while on a sandbagged wall."

"Glittering stars in a black velvet sky,
Blaze like gems in the tranquil night,
And breezes soft as a baby's sigh
Bear no danger with the fading light."

Brief those moments may have been
However, they did indeed exist.
Peaceful time spent with friends,
Away from war's inhuman fist.

So, take the time to search them out
From where you've hidden them away;
They're still there, without a doubt
Ready to soothe and brighten your day.

Look deep within, I'm sure you'll find,
Green and bright and dappled with sun,
That peaceful corner in your mind...
I know that God made more than one.

© 2/23/2002 Thurman P. Woodfork
Dedicated to Garland Young, who, at
times, grows weary of sad songs.
~~~

Memorial Day - Summer Begins

A moment's pause by Grandma's grave,
Then a heartfelt salute for those who gave
Their all in one of the many wars
And departed this life on some foreign shore.

Let's leave a rose for Daddy dear,
And bless Mama's stone with a jeweled tear.
The memories are warm on this special day
Of the Dearly Beloved who have gone away.

With a final sigh, our duties are done,
A glance at our watch tells us we must run
To catch the sales at our favorite shops
And then prepare the ribs and chops

For the usual gala holiday cookout.
Isn't that what this day is really all about?
~~~

The Weary GI Blues
Sittin' here and sighin' at the tops of my shoes
'Cause the day's already colored in dark and somber
hues. I wonder just how long I'll keep payin' these
dues: I got the low-down, dirty, Weary GI blues.

Over twenty years travelin' from one site to another,
Only to discover that one's just like the other;
From Mississippi's Gulf shore to Alaska north of
Nome
I've set down my duffel bag and made myself at
home.

Sittin' here sighin' at the tops of my shoes
'Cause the day's already colored in dark and somber
hues.
I wonder just how long I'll keep payin' these dues:
I got the low-down, dirty, Wanderin' GI Blues.

Perched on this mountaintop in Spain south of
France,
Thinkin' about Barcelona and sweet, Latin romance;
But it's in between paydays and my pockets are all
bare
And the chaplain's stopped the travel chits that used
to get me there.

Sittin' here sighin' at the tops of my shoes
'Cause the day's already colored in dark and somber
hues.
I wonder just how long I'll keep payin' these dues:
I got the low-down, dirty, Horny GI Blues.

Sweet Jesus, there's a Dragon in the night sky
overhead
Belching deadly metal fire that's neon bright and
red!
It really is named Puff and it's beautiful to behold...
But not to the Viet Cong whose bodies are turning
cold.

Sittin' here sighin' at the tops of my shoes

'Cause the day's already colored in dark and somber hues.
I wonder just how long I'll keep payin' these dues:
I got the low-down, dirty, Cold Soul GI Blues.

Another Mountain in Korea, now there's snow up to my ass,
Mumblin' to myself, "Lord, how long can this shit last?"
Musin' on the perfidy of folks I thought were friends,
Lookin' towards the DMZ as another long day ends.

Sittin' here sighin' at the tops of my shoes
'Cause the day's already colored in dark and somber hues.
I wonder just how long I'll keep payin' these dues:
I got the low-down, dirty, Frostbit GI Blues.

Well, now active duty is over and retirement time is here,
Can I lie back on my laurels sippin' San Miguel beer -
Dreamin' 'bout the Ramblas and sweet songs like Twilight Time?
Nope, this stingy GI pension won't buy no life sublime.

Sittin' here sighin' at the tops of my shoes
'Cause the day's already colored in dark and somber hues.
I wonder just how long I'll keep payin' these dues:
I got the low-down, dirty, Disillusioned GI Blues.

What happened to that promise of free lifetime medical care?
Congress slowly took it back 'til now there's nothing there.
It's, "What've you done for me lately, and that's for damn' sure.
Yep, it's supplemental insurance 'cause the wolf's at the door.

Sittin' here sighin' at the tops of my shoes

'Cause the day's already colored in dark and somber
hues.
I wonder just how long I'll keep payin' these dues:
I got the low-down, dirty, Back-Stabbed GI Blues.
~~~

Flashback

There he sits as usual,
alone with his innermost thoughts;
these days he's content to be alone;
no other company is sought.
No wife's homey chatter, no noisy kids' clatter,
only the blessed quiet
that surrounds him on the outside,
but now, in his head, there's a riot.

Noisy, whirling chopper blades
join chattering, clattering guns
as he groans and curses the darkness,
praying for the morning sun.
Then Spooky's flares turn the night to noon,
as with a whirring roar,
a red tongue of tracers licks hungrily down,
searching the jungle floor.

The enemy retreats on silent feet,
ghosting away through the trees,
while the choking smoke gradually floats
away on the drifting breeze.
But suddenly, he sees that there are no trees,
no underbrush, nor any leaves,
just the rumbling tanks advancing in ranks
through clouds of sand on TV.

So, he suppresses a sigh, blinks rueful eyes,
aims the remote control,
and with a firm, gentle press of his finger,
retains his hold on his soul.

(Dedicated to C. D., who had a sort of epiphany.)

Stored Boxes

A box of mementos stored away on a shelf;
Remnants and souvenirs of an earlier self
Conjure up memories of times gone by
Brought into focus by the mind's eye...

Inanimate objects, yet possessed of a power
To evoke sweet memories of a lover's flower
Still jeweled with drops from a gentle shower -
Or recall red blossoms from a deadly watchtower

In an isolated jungle camp in a long ago war
And flick the scab from an unhealed sore.
As with Pandora's chest, one might come to find
That it's best not to open some boxes in the mind.
~~~

Helping Hands

I read my friend's anguish with pained heart -
stark words on a monitor screen bleeding living grief
-
and search for words of my own to ease the hurting,
to offer some measure of relief.

I wonder why they are so slow to come,
these words, so laggard in forming when
the glib responses used to be so quickly done:
they rolled so easily off my tongue.

It's as if such eloquent pain mutes
and shames my response by the depth of its
intensity. Its genuineness demands an
equally honest passion in reply.

This is real pain, palpable sorrow, pure regret,
an almost unbearable desire to alter that
which can't be changed, what is forever absolute.

How do I ease this amalgam of emotions...
grief, anger, bone deep sorrow, mixed with
just a little shame and an aching, endless feeling
of loss? The need to Just Stop Remembering,
if only for today. What can I say?

And I read on, the words of comfort aching -
stillborn in my brain, momentarily unable to
energize the quiescent fingers of my hands
resting futilely on the keyboard...
Helpless...helpless.

For Bruce 'Doc' Melson
~~

That Which We Call a Boot

Boots, boots, many sorts of boots
I've worn all kinds, usually those that would suit
The job that I was assigned at the time,
And as far as I'm concerned, that was just fine.

They ranged from combat to the safety ones,
Because, in my job, I didn't require a gun,
I did need boots that would prevent a shock
Of electricity from suddenly stopping my clock.

I employed electrons in my war, you see -
I didn't hunt Charlie, he came looking for me.
But, sometimes I had to do a quick flip
From working on the radar to make a fast trip

To the perimeter wall for my machine gun
And help yank a knot in Charlie's fun.
Since I rarely traveled very far on my feet,
To engage the enemy - or in prudent retreat -

I rarely thought about those boots of mine,
Mostly, they were just something to shine.
~~~

Homecoming Festival

I have witnessed festivals all over the world
From the Bulls of Pamplona to the glittering swirl
Of the crowds in New Orleans on Mardi Gras Day.
And they all were impressive, each in its way.

But, by far the most impressive of all
Wasn't on a foreign plaza or the DC Mall.
It was the heartfelt joy of a dear old friend
Saying, "I'm glad you're safely home again."

But what of the men who will never see
Glad faces like the ones that welcomed me;
Men who for thirty long years and more
Have been locked behind their captors' doors?

There are some who'd rather turn away
And forget those men who were willing to pay
With their lives and their youth for democracy.
Weren't those men also fighting to stay free?

Observe the politicians who were never there
To fight for their country and really don't care
That some who did have never come home -
That they've been abandoned to suffer alone;

They speak of patriotism with puffed up chests
While surreptitiously feathering their nests.
Our forsaken men surely wonder why
Their country has callously left them to die.

Bleak yesterdays become hopeless tomorrows,
With nothing ahead but more days of sorrow,
What do they care about pageantry
And homecoming festivals across the sea?

So, shall we just shrug and let them be
A shameful footnote in our history?
~~~

Bunkered Up

If you're weary of hiding and can no longer run,
then leave your bunker and come out into the sun;
abandon that ultimately useless drink
in favor of someone that you think
Is worthy of your trust.

Confess the hidden fears that combust
and inflame those recurring dreams
that shatter your sleep with mental screams.
Tell of the things that sear your soul
and ignite the anger, flaring hot then cold.

Stop saying, "You just won't understand,"
forcing loved ones to raise their hands
and leave you to wrestle all alone
with demons that creep into your very bones.

Do it: do it and you may find surcease
from haunting memories and gain release
from the anguish of pain unexpressed

that rends the heart twisted in your chest
by the agonizing, secret memories you keep.

Vomit it up, purge your soul and sleep.
~~~

Baffled Tiger

From shadowy greenery, about to unfold
Into dappled sunlight, flashing gold,
Erupts a horrific roar of murderous sounds.
Chattering rifles and mortar rounds

Explode the quiet into death and screams.
As sunbeams dance, glitter and gleam
From bleeding flesh and shattered bone,
Bodies fall, quiver, and moan.

Not far away a tiger holds still
Crouched above her freshly caught kill.
When the fury of the nearby fray
Shudders to an end and fades away,

She cautiously sniffs the ominous air
Then quietly ghosts away from there.
As the sound of distant choppers rise
She glances back with wondering eyes.

The sophisticated ways of men
Are far beyond her feral ken.
~~~

If Only I Were Twenty Again

If only I were twenty again,
I'd do all the things I neglected then:
I'd learn quantum physics with alacrity
And go Adventuring Across the Seas.

Yes, I'd paint a stunning masterpiece,
Then find 'The Lost Star of the East'.
I'd even harness the power of the sun,
If only I were twenty-one.

Then off to La Scala for a bravura turn
Donating to charity the millions I'd earn.
I'd conquer disease and poverty forever
And forge a peace no nation could sever.

I'd unite the world in harmony
Long before I was twenty-three.
I'd enthrall the house at the Bolshoi Ballet
And earn a Tony the very next day.

I'd win the World Series for DC once more
And whip the Heavyweight Champ in four.
Just think of the wondrous things I could do
...If only I were twenty-two.
~~~

The Sentinel?

What is causing the palpable unease of this man who sits alone in solitary, forced calmness? It's evident that there's no serenity in his silence.

His brooding eyes are now turned inward, momentarily blind to the living here and now that surrounds him. He's lost in a somber reverie of long ago sights and sounds – past events that are very much part of his present.

What is he watching for from deep within the psychic bunker of his mind as he fitfully rises to patrol its intangible perimeter? What immutable sorrow is he holding almost tenderly to himself while yet wishing it gone?

If he really is hiding, why does he never turn off the lights? No matter how intense, they can't illuminate or relieve the gloom that waits just beyond their brightness to envelop him like the melancholy shadow of Poe's raven.

But he really isn't alone. Deep within that pensive darkness, almost unseen, lies a smoldering, illusive presence, coiled and also watching.

So, does this sequestered, conflicted soul seek to reject the world, or is he actually protecting those who're locked outside his self-imposed, invisible barrier?

Unanswered questions that only give rise to even more speculation. He has become a living, enigmatic, ineffable...sigh.
~~~

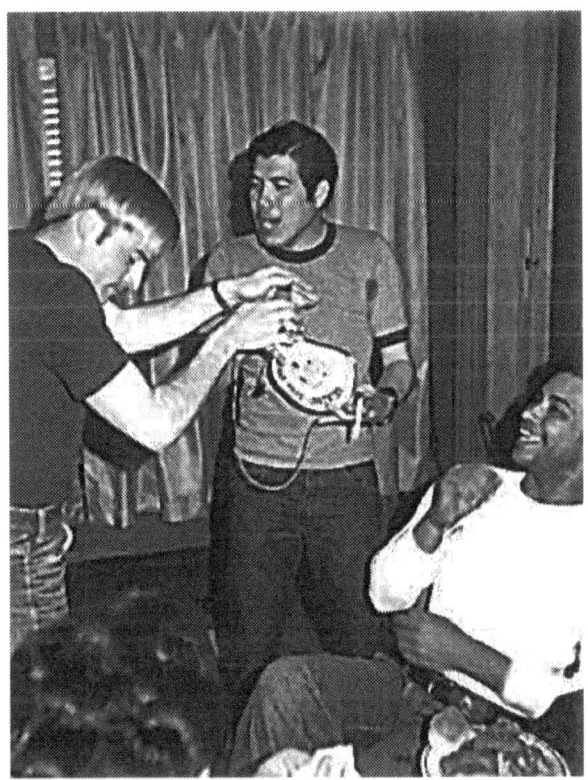

My Choice

Fondly viewed through my mind's eye,
Ever youthful, ever spry,
Live those friends of bygone days,
Full of pranks and cheerful ways.

Were we really so carefree,
Or is it that I prefer to see
Them ambling down my memory's lane
Free of sorrow, free from pain?

Why hold on to life's grim parts;
Why not recall the lighter hearts?
After all, I can choose
To paint my past in somber hues

Or dip my brush in summer sun
And make my landscapes bright with fun.
Yes, I think - just for today -
I will use no shades of gray.

It's enough that, when I sleep,
I hear voices softly weep.
~~~

Baggage

One year out of twenty five -
thirty five years gone - pursues,
haunts and hangs on me so,
won't let me go...Never a day
goes by that some memory
does not return, unbidden,
unwanted...Waiting for an
unguarded moment to slither
stealthily into my consciousness
and coil there...smug, beady-
eyed, coolly triumphant in
all its odiousness. Knowing
that the blink of an eye or an
angry headshake will again
banish it to the darkness
whence it came, but also
knowing that it can return
at any moment my mind is
idle...any moment now.
~~~

Season's Greetings

Christmas: jingle bells and holly,
Santa Claus so round and jolly,
Cheerful songs and sparkling snow
Fragrant trees and candle glow.

Children's eyes wide with wonder
As they survey their yearly plunder
Everyone filled with peace and love
And gentle blessings from above.

Over Iraq deadly birds soar
War ships ride at anchor off shore
For the moment we sing the hymn
Of peace on earth, good will to men.
~~~

Realists, God, and War

There will never be an end
To war's recurrent hell
While 'realists' shrug their shoulders,
With a fatalistic "Oh well."

"There are no gods to help you;
You only pray in vain;
So raise your children in anticipation
Of going to war again."

"Just cover up your heads
And don't even bother to try
For that's the way life must be
Beneath these godless skies."

Tell me, is there a difference
if I do nothing more than pray,
Or sit in mute acceptance
Of whatever comes my way?

For those who don't believe in God,
I say that is their right,
But please do not discourage me
From reaching for His light.

For I have chosen to believe
And there's nothing I will say
To alter their chosen paths
Traveling through life's days.

If I am wrong, when life ends
Then what have I really lost?
If they are wrong at the end,
It's they who'll pay the cost.

Protestations of Peace

One cannot protest slaughter
With words of sweet accord:
Peace often needs strong arms
Wielding finely honed swords.

But never forget that words are
The mightiest weapons of all,
Their insidious influence is able
To hold entire nations in thrall.

We are not moved to battle
By gentle words of peace -
Can entreaties softly uttered
Cause roaring guns to cease?

I will not whisper 'Peace'
Like a cooing turtle dove;
When the carnage has ended,
Then speak to me of love.

I'll thunder to the heavens
Of my anguish and my pain
Until the gods relent and send
Peace back to me again.
~~~

Memories and a Visit

Recently, I heard from Marty Martinez, an old friend I had not spoken with in years. We had been stationed on El Pani, a mountain in Spain that held the small radar squadron to which we were assigned. Our reunion was bittersweet; Marty told me that our old friend, Max, died a few years ago. Max had been one of the medics on Pani.

And so, another friend has lost the counterfeit immortality of youth and gone to join friends and family who made this inevitable transition before him. It makes me stop and think about things that had never concerned me before. I look at my brothers and sisters, who have gradually grown grey and less nimble over the years, and contemplate life without them. Until recently, my friends had died as the result of wars and accidents; now, the summons is "Natural Causes."

I think of old friends I have not contacted for years, although they live in the same city; that's easily corrected. I think, with regret, of other old friends I'd made in far away places - other cities and foreign countries - with whom I've lost contact through careless neglect...letters that were allowed to go unanswered. Finally, the letters stopped coming. Not so easy to correct.

Today, a neighbor came to the door; she just wanted to say that she would still be our neighbor. As I stood and watched her slow progress back to her own home, I recalled when she and her husband had first moved next door, over fifty years ago.

Her husband, a daughter, and a son have all passed away; she is now enfeebled and her memory is a little uncertain. I wondered what prompted her to come and announce that she would still be our neighbor. She finally reached her door and went inside. I heard her door close behind her and closed my own. I hope her visit was not a portent of a less welcome caller.

Some folks say that a person lives on as long as his or her memory survives. It occurs to me that this sentiment is only valid if one doesn't believe in the soul's immortality. When their last friend, relative, or acquaintance dies, those who had gone before would blink out along with them. Not a happy idea to mull over.
~~~

Sex in Saigon

I'm sitting in a bar in Saigon, wearing civilian clothes. If one ignores the fact that all the women are Asian, I could be in a GI bar almost anywhere in the world.

Well, that, and the loaded .45 tucked in my waistband behind my belt. Aside from that reminder, in here, the war seems far off. It's easy to let the mind slip away; I've been in many similar bars.

A young lady slides in beside me and begins the ancient, time honored, professional seduction - for want of a better term, since I'm hardly being seduced. We argue amiably and desultorily, first over the price of the Saigon Tea and then over what I maintain is an equally exorbitant price for sex before I give in and accompany her.

We enter a huge room, and here, the familiarity ends: The room is filled with rows of precisely aligned cots covered with white, gauze-like mosquito netting. Dimly seen figures are gyrating under the netting in the timeless motions of 'love.' I undress and climb onto the cot under my own netting with the girl, slipping the .45 under the pillow, unobtrusively, I hoped.

But it's no good...too surreal...the rows of ghostly, white-shrouded beds make me think of a casualty ward, or worse. The gun, inches from my hand, adds to the unreality of the scene. Coupled with the occupied, spectral cots on every side of me, it's too disconcerting. Eventually, I give up and start to dress again, which is quickly done, since I don't wear underclothing, in deference to the climate.

This time, I make no effort to conceal the gun as I tuck it back under my shirt. The girl only offers a token protest; she's undoubtedly glad for the respite. She remains there under the netting as I make my way back past the ghostly files of shrouded cots and out to the street. The next day, I'm back on Trang Sup, and it is all like a half-remembered dream.

~~~

Absent Demons

What is this vague but unrelenting discontent? When did ambition quietly slip away and leave gentle despair in its place? Talents languish undeveloped waiting for tomorrow as tomorrow plods wearily on to become today, then fades unexploited into yesterday. Aspirations molder away like once favored toys now tossed into a corner to lie neglected and forgotten. Where did this deep, abiding, banked anger come from? Will it ever leave?

Now, after a reunion, there is the unsettling memory of an old friend smiling in happy surprise: "I think that's the first time I've ever heard you really laugh." Seeing me regularly for five and often six days a week, how could he not have heard me laugh? I'm left wondering if that could possibly be true. He never heard me really laugh even once in three years? If it is true, why should it be?

For there are no disturbing memories that trouble my waking hours; no demons come unbidden in the night to disrupt my dreamless sleep - if I finally do go to sleep. I only know that I want something that I realize is obtainable but that I cannot muster enough caring to reach for and grasp. Why is that? When did spring come and go without my caring or even acknowledging it?

I have always loved the smell of spring as the earth awakens and renews itself. Now spring has come and gone, summer is here and the rose bushes remain untended. "How can it be summer when I am in the winter of my discontent?" I've come to understand what that misquoted bit of Shakespeare means, and not even reuniting with old friends can ease this malaise. Bleak and barren is what I feel, and suicide is not an option.

So, I will bear it as I have borne it for all these long, weary years. And only a few people will ever realize - as I now do - that, although I smile a lot, I seldom ever really laugh.

But then...there are no demons.
~~~

Nam Thoughts

I wonder how many Viet Nam vets there are like me who seem to have escaped the mental trauma of having served in that nastiness. True, I was a technician who remained in the relative safety of a camp but still, something feels amiss: why don't I feel more than I do about Viet Nam? It's not that I want to feel unhappy; it's just that I can't help feeling a little guilty at times for having seemingly returned relatively unscathed.

When I consider that it was certainly like no other period in my life, surely I should feel something more about it, some deeper emotions, or, at least remember more about day to day events than I do. I've never had a flashback, hell I never even have any dreams about the place that I know of, but that's not strange, because I don't seem to dream about anything anymore.

Well, the truth is that I do dream, it's simply that I never recall what the dreams are about. And I usually dream in color, which should at least make the dreams more vivid and memorable. When I consciously think of Viet Nam, it's without rancor or hatred. I bear the Vietnamese no malice, although some of them did most assiduously try to shorten my time here on Planet Earth.

Even so, I'm more likely to recall something that was amusing rather than something ominous. I seem to remember more about the much more tranquil parts of my military career than I do about the turbulence of that year I spent at war. It doesn't seem logical.

In Viet Nam, I was much more aware of my surroundings; my senses were more sharply tuned, surely I should remember more of what they recorded, but I do not. I can watch a movie or read books about Viet Nam without any seeming emotional involvement, but I have not been inside a movie theater since I left the Philippine Islands in 1969. My tour of duty in Viet Nam was over in 1967.

I remember the pain when my brother died - the person I loved most in the world. He was nineteen and I was seventeen, and I was with him when he died. Nearly thirty years passed before I wept for him. Maybe, once again, I've just buried the unwelcome thoughts somewhere in my subconscious mind. Perhaps I just have a few more years to wait before Viet Nam begins to rise up. I don't think so, though. I didn't love Viet Nam.

~~~

Dehumanizing the Enemy

I was explaining to some friends how I didn't get the "Dehumanizing the Enemy" indoctrination before I went to Nam when I remembered an incident that happened in Tay Ninh City when I wandered away from my friends. It was late in the afternoon and I was in a small jewelry shop looking around when these two little Vietnamese teenagers came in. They scowled at me and one of them slapped the butt of my loaded rifle as he passed behind me. The rifle was slung over my shoulder, and I probably shouldn't have let them walk behind me, but they were so little - I easily outweighed both of them together with pounds to spare - and so young looking that I didn't really feel any danger.

At any rate, with a few glowers over their shoulders, they continued on their way through the shop and disappeared through a door at the back. The proprietor, who had been very affable up until then, suddenly became agitated and nervous and urged me to leave, saying, "You go now," because he had to close up. First time I ever saw a Vietnamese back away from a potential sale. I left and he closed and locked the door almost before I got outside, so I took my dumb ass back to the truck where the others were waiting.

When I related what had just happened to me, I was told I was lucky that all those two innocent looking "kids" had done was slap my M-16. They could just as easily have slipped a knife into one of my kidneys when they walked behind my unsuspecting, unprotected back, and made off with the weapons and ammo that I carried. God does indeed have a soft spot for babies and fools.

Chalk it up to the drawbacks of a sparse two weeks of training, with no "dehumanizing" of the enemy. All the Vietnamese folks I had seen during daylight hours, up until then, had always been smiling and friendly. It finally occurred to me that some of them were not all that happy about the fact that big, oversized Nimnulls like me were in their country and that they had probably been through some "Dehumanizing the Enemy" indoctrination of their own.
~~~

Vietnam

I arrived in the Republic of South Vietnam on 11 July 1966 and remained until 5 July 1967, when I was reassigned PCS to Clark Air Force Base in the Philippines. For years, I thought that I had arrived in Vietnam in May of 1965; then, I thought it was June of '66. I finally learned the correct dates from records received from the National Personnel Records Center in St. Louis, MO. Lord knows why I couldn't remember the correct dates on my own.

I do recall now that a friend, Esther Smith, had given me a small going away picnic on or about the Fourth of July down at Haines Point in DC, near where The Wall is now. How could I forget these things?

I spent some time in 'Tent City' on Tan Son Nhut waiting for assignment. That time, too is dimmed but I remember going into Saigon several times with some Air Policemen who were waiting to go somewhere upcountry. I think maybe they were going to Cam Rahn Bay, but I won't swear to it. There was a Master Sergeant with them who was, shall we say, unhappy with the delay.

Finally, I received my assignment to Detachment 7, 619th Tactical Control Squadron, located in Tay Ninh Province. I was directed to a helicopter pad where I could catch a ride to my new home. Det. 7 was located on Trang-Sup, an Army Special Forces camp; which I didn't learn until I got on the helicopter.

We landed in Tay Ninh West, and I rode out to Trang-Sup in the back of a six-by. When we got there, I saw a couple of Americans wearing fatigue pants and T-shirts, or no shirts at all, and a whole bunch of little Vietnamese people who promptly started patting and stroking me. I had no idea what they were saying, but I was certainly glad that they appeared to be so friendly.

I asked one of my new companions if all new arrivals got greeted like that, and he said it was the first time he'd seen it. I later decided that it was my shiny new starched and pressed synthetic fiber fatigues my friendly reception committee was admiring and not my extraordinarily virile physique, magnificent though it was. Another ego buster.

There were about thirty-five Americans on Trang-Sup, and a whole slew of Vietnamese and some Cambodians who the Special Forces people were training. At first, it was hard to tell the Air Force from the Army, since nobody seemed to be wearing shirts or hats. It took a few days to get them all sorted out.

I was assigned as a long range radar repairman, my job was to help repair and maintain the AN/UPS-1 radar set. This turned out to be a tiny (to me) ground-transportable Marine radar entirely housed in a room about the size of an average living room. I was accustomed to huge, sprawling, multi-storied set-ups. The modulator cabinet at my last site was about as big as this entire UPS-1 (pronounced Yoopsy One). So there I was: an Airman assigned to maintain a Marine radar set in an Army camp. All that was missing was a boat.

Trang-Sup was about fifty-five miles northwest of Saigon and approximately twenty miles from the Cambodian border. Tay Ninh city, the province capital, was eight or nine miles south of Trang-Sup. One thing very quickly became obvious: the camp was, as a rule, miraculously devoid of indigenous civilian personnel on those occasions when we had unwelcome visitors. Made one sort of wonder just how many Viet Cong, or their sympathizers, were actually already inside the camp on a daily basis.

The camp itself was located in one of the old forts left behind by the French, a bunch of green trimmed white buildings arranged in a large rectangle. The Army guys lived in one building, called the Team House, which commanded an unobstructed view of the camp. The Air Force enlisted people occupied an adjacent building that at one time had been an open bay barracks. It had been divided into rooms that were actually cubicles; the top and bottom thirds of the inner walls were screened.

The dispensary, Air Force orderly room and officer's quarters, radar operations and radio maintenance were in a building directly across and about three long strides from the enlisted men's barracks. Radar maintenance was in a separate small building behind Ops and was mercifully air conditioned, as was Ops. Had to keep all that electronic gear running. Well, anyway, there I was; home at last...home, at least, for the next year.

~~~

A Memory

I was watching the TV show 'Boston Common' one night, and Roberta Flack's *"Killing Me Softly"* was an integral part of the plot. Once again, half-forgotten memories came stealing softly back unbidden from the recesses of my mind. Tay Ninh, with Nui Ba Den brooding in the distance, the dimly remembered but unmistakable aroma of Trai Trang-Sup and Vietnam...

This song always makes me think of Vietnam whenever I hear it. My good friend, Larry Moore, was a pretty fair country guitar player, but I had long been out of Vietnam, indeed, away from SEA for a couple of years before I ever heard the song. For a long time, I didn't occur to me that I could be subconsciously thinking of him.

Perhaps I was put off by the lines: "And there he was, this young boy; a stranger to my eyes, strumming my pain..." Larry was my best friend there, and hardly a stranger; and he certainly never caused me any pain other than worry when he went on patrol. But I can see him now, sitting in his hooch or in our little club, or perched on the sand bags, strumming his guitar and singing.

~~~

Lyman Rigby

Larry

I came to love him, my friend Larry from West Virginia. Actually, his name is Richard, Richard Moore, but he preferred to be called Larry, not Dick or Rich or Rick. I know that he told me the reason once, but I've forgotten; most likely his middle name was Lawrence. Larry was a Green Beret, a small, slender young man in excellent condition. He was very agile and very lithe; he could stand in a doorway and effortlessly kick the lintel directly above his head without losing his balance.

Even after I got to know him well I could never quite reconcile the warrior at his deadly business off on patrol in the dense green jungle with this gentle kid who loved to play the guitar and sing. He somehow got left down in Tay Ninh one evening and walked the eight or nine miles back to Trang-Sup alone in the dark. He was carrying a .45 automatic and an M-16 and had a grease gun slung down his back. I asked him why he hadn't gone to the B Team in Tay Ninh to spend the night and he looked at me expressionlessly and said, "Because I don't belong to B Team; I belong here." I had no response to that. Actually, I felt a little stupid for having asked. Apparently, he didn't care that Charlie was supposed to own the night.

I would wait for them to come back from one of their forays into the jungle and pretend that I wasn't really concerned during his absence. It was as if to actively worry would somehow bring on some unseen calamity. I did say something once, and he laughed, punched me lightly in the chest and asked if I wanted to come along next time and hold his hand. He once said that he would prefer to have me with him than any of the Vietnamese troops who accompanied him and his teammates on their hazardous trips across the paddies and through the jungle. He said that to me even though I was an Air Force Zoomie not trained for combat. I was inordinately pleased, although I contrived to hide it.

We were an unlikely pair, the Green Beret grunt and the Air Force radar repairman; he was in his early twenties, and I was thirty-one. I was always mildly astonished that we had become such close friends and often wondered why he had singled me out, although I was content to accept his companionship and never asked. I also could never tell him how much I valued his friendship; I was somehow certain that if I did, something bad would surely happen to him. He had already been wounded twice.

Sometimes when he was in camp we would sit together in his hooch room while he strummed at his guitar and sang softly, half to himself. We could sit that way for a long time without talking. At other times we would sit up on top of the sandbags surrounding one of the mortar pits near the perimeter fence and talk about everything and nothing. We embraced once; we had been sitting on the mortar pit and jumped down to go back into the main part of camp. Without speaking, he suddenly put his arms around my neck. Surprised, I put my arms around him and we stood there silently for a moment, then we turned and walked back as though nothing had passed between us. But I knew that I would always be his friend as long as I lived

He left eventually, shipped out to another camp, and I never saw him again. There was some mildly superstitious concern over his leaving because it was rumored that the last three camps he'd left had been over-run within a month of his departure. I suppose that in our case, the fourth time was the charm, because nothing that bad happened to us although we did get attacked. When my year was up, I went to 5th TAC in the Philippines.

I had his sister's address in West Virginia, and when I finally returned to the States three and a half years after leaving for SEA (Southeast Asia), I wrote to her planning to visit. But she didn't respond and I didn't write again. I checked The Wall and his name is not there, so at least I know that Larry made it back. I wonder if he ever thinks of me; I have never forgotten him, but while I am now sixty-six, he's still in his twenties, in my mind's eye.
~~~

©2001 T.P. Woodfork, Det. 7, 619th TCS 1966-1967

Watching the War

So, there I was in Vietnam. After eleven years in the service, I finally wound up in a war zone. I arrived fresh from radar installations in northern Montana - Cut Bank and Lewistown, to be precise - not fully knowing what to expect. My presence in War Zone C had almost as much to do with boredom as it did with patriotism. Cut Bank Air Force Station, for example, was forty-four miles from the city of Cut Bank, a town of some two thousand citizens. It was a great place for a city boy like me to be stationed. All my hunting and fishing had been done in concrete canyons.

Prior to leaving the States for Nam, the Air Force had given me a two-week course in California on the M-16, hand grenade throwing, and probably some other stuff that I don't remember now. Then they sent me on my merry way to the Land of the Ao Dai. Combat trainin'? What combat trainin'? I was a radar repairman; I didn't need no stinkin' combat trainin'! And I didn't get much, either. The Special Forces guys had to take me in hand once I showed up in their camp.

After all, I wasn't supposed to be doing any serious grunt-type fighting, that's what the Army and Marines are for; I was a technician. The SF troops did a better job of teaching us, anyway. We learned how to use all the weapons in camp, from mortars to the venerable .45 automatic. Oscilloscopes and multimeters make piss-poor weapons in a firefight.

Initially, I found myself in an interesting situation on Trang-Sup; I was in Vietnam, but the war was on the periphery of my existence; it was something happening elsewhere to somebody else. Except for obvious things like sandbagged walls, barbed wire, mortar emplacements, and the more primitive living conditions, I could almost have been back on one of those remote Montana radar sites. I got up each morning, greeted Nui Ba Den brooding in the near distance, and went to work on the radar. In the evenings, I hung out at the little club or around the barracks.

Oh, and the heat; don't forget that - or the smothering humidity. Northern Montana never even dreamed of anything close to Vietnam's sauna-like heat. I was told that the camp itself was an old French fort left over from the days of French Indo-China. The towers at the corners of the camp, plus the one in the center, also served as a reminder of where I was and what I could look forward to. The most dangerous thing I'd had to worry about in Montana was accidentally electrocuting myself, or maybe surprising a grumpy bear on an evening garbage can raid. The dangerous creatures here also usually waited for the dark of night to begin their activities, only they were far more deadly than the bears. Not to mention better armed.

For the first few weeks, life went along uneventfully as I became accustomed to the camp routine. Sergeant of the Guard was occasionally diverting, though; the Vietnamese counterpart would appear on the hour to accompany the American on his inspection trip around the perimeter. The night was livened up when we found somebody asleep, which was usually the case. The little Vietnamese NCO would sometimes proceed to do a tap dance on the offending troop. After the first few times, I pretended not to notice anything unusual about an NCO routinely kicking the shit out of a subordinate.

The perimeter guards were usually dressed in black. I had thought only Charlie was supposed to wear those black pajama type outfits, but here, even the Americans sometimes wore them. The GIs usually wore the black PJs more for comfort while in camp than for anything else.

As I said, those first weeks at Trang-Sup passed almost without incident. At night, we sometimes sat on a sandbagged wall and "watched the war" off in the distance. The far away rumble of detonating ordinance pointed up the flashes from explosions and tracer fire. The tracers look like distant fireflies dancing about the darkness as aircraft pressed the attack. Flares washed the tracers from the night, and then slowly sank below the horizon like a descending stage curtain as the lights went down and the scene faded to black as the attack ended.

Two West Virginians - an Airman named White and an Army Special Forces guy named Larry Moore – sometimes brought their guitars out and we would sing along as they played. Being an indifferent pianist, I had to admire their skillful musicianship. Once, when I had trouble singing, *"Where Have All the Flowers Gone,"* because I didn't know the words, a helpful lieutenant obligingly fed me each line. He jokingly said that I sang much better than he did anyway. It was all rather surreal. There I was, perched on sandbags in Vietnam and singing protest songs, the lyrics of which were being supplied to me by an officer. Fantastic.

Then, one night, I awoke to the chunk of mortars exploding outside and the insistent sound of the alarms. A rather sickly siren and a loud, strident ringing like an angry, uninterrupted, old-fashioned telephone bell were announcing that the war was no longer just on the horizon; the vacation was over. I had, instantly and permanently, switched from interested observer to active participant. On my way to my machine gun, I heard humming sounds which, I realized with a shock, meant that bullets were passing unnervingly close to me.

Once inside the pitch-black machine gun bunker, I strained to see out the gun port. My companion muttered, "I wonder if there are any snakes in here." I considered throttling him; I hate snakes. I had not been in the bunker at night before. The war was now sitting and watching me, and the song it was singing was about Death.

~~~

The First Attack

This is a story about the fear that I, an Air Force radar repairman with minimal combat training, felt when I experienced my first enemy attack and realized that I really could be killed, and my deep relief when it didn't happen and I emerged unscathed when it was over.

The Alarm! We're under attack! Charlie is here! I grab my rifle and snatch my pack from its place on the wall. Breathing fast, I run quickly to my position behind the Commo bunker. Crouched under the sandbags, I load the machine gun with hurrying, anxious fingers, meanwhile trying to peer through the dark opening into the featureless blackness beyond the bunker. There had been a flurry of small arms fire to the right of my position, but now it's quiet.

There's nothing to see. Where are they? How far away are they? How close are they? It is so damned dark! There's nothing to see, nothing to see. But I know they're out there, quiet, invisible, menacing. I keep scanning the darkness. I should have stayed back on my radar site in Montana, bored but safe. Well, I'm damned sure not bored now.

Man, it's dark. Long forgotten childhood memories start to surface. I remember lying concealed in the basement back on Third Street in DC, playing hide and seek on a summer evening, but this is no game. These are no friendly neighborhood kids searching the night here, but an implacable enemy intent on my destruction. My heart is beating fast and heavy as I feel I can detect the menace beyond the wire. I know that there are friends all around me; there's a guy right beside me, but I feel constricted, isolated by the sandbags. I keep straining to see. How can it be so dark? Two weeks training for this. Shit! Then someone is behind me at the bunker entrance.

Bac Si Cox, the Army Special Forces medic, is a dimly seen smile and an easy voice, asking: "How's it going?" "Okay so far, Danny," I answer, surprised that my lowered voice sounds almost normal. "Hey, man, don't mean nothin'..." he says, as he detects the suppressed emotion. We talk softly for a few seconds, and then he leaves as quietly as he came.

After he's gone, I realize that my heartbeat has returned almost to normal. Reassured, I peer at the shadowy figure of the guy hunkered close beside me in the bunker and wonder why I did not draw comfort from his presence as I did with Danny.

My bunker mate's a few years older than my thirty-one. Danny Cox must be nearly ten years younger than I am, but in experience, he is my grandfather. After a few more almost desultory scattered shots, it's over. It seems that Charlie really wasn't serious in his attack this time. After having left us in peace for so long, he just wanted to remind us that he is still out there. Point taken: the night belongs to him. As far as I'm concerned, he can have it.

There is a further wait, then we're told to hang it up. We secure the machine gun and leave the bunker. I breathe a long, long, silent sigh. My first attack is over and I am still very much alive.

~~~

"The End is Not Yet"

And ye shall hear of wars and rumors of wars: see that ye be not troubled: for all [these things] must come to pass, but the end is not yet. -- Mathew 24:6

My Children, be ye of good cheer;
The end may not be so near.
We have fretted for years,
Filled ourselves with fears
Of dire things to come,
An excuse for some
To foment war,
Saying Christ himself foresaw
This endless cycle of pain
As war comes again and again
When He meant only to reassure
And not excuse more
Eternally recurring war.
Judgment awaits warmongers,
The rapacious ones who hunger,
With riches and power their creed
As they plot to satisfy their sinful needs.

And He shall judge among the nations, and shall rebuke many people: and they shall beat their swords into plowshares, and their spears into pruning hooks: nation shall not lift up sword against nation; neither shall they learn war any more. -- Isaiah 2:4

~~~

Trai Trang-Sup Village

In 1966-67 I was stationed in a Special Force Camp called Trang-Sup outside of Tay Ninh City. The camp was located in what had once been a French fort. I was an Air Force long-range radar repairman attached to Det. 7 of the 619th Tactical Control Squadron, Call Sign "Penthouse. One inky night, a large enemy force surrounded our camp. Their purpose was not to attack the military personnel in the camp, but rather the families of some of the Vietnamese military assigned to the camp. These families lived in the village of Trang-Sup just outside the camp perimeter. Charlie wanted to prevent the Special Forces people and their South Vietnamese counterparts from coming to the rescue of the villagers, and they succeeded.

After surrounding us, they methodically mortared and raked the village with small arms fire, finally setting it ablaze while we remained bottled up in camp. The phrase 'with malice aforethought' aptly applies to this act of calculated, cold-blooded murder. It seemed to last for hours while we watched from the camp in frustrated anger and anguish, but it was really all over in a few short minutes. The VC knowingly and deliberately killed innocent women, children and old people with one purpose in mind: terrorize and punish them and their military family members for being aligned with the governments of South Vietnam and the United States. Their message was that, although we were within spitting distance, we could be neutralized long enough for them to create havoc and get away.

I have no firsthand knowledge of atrocities that may have been committed by the U.S. military or their allies in Vietnam, but I personally witnessed this particular act of icily detached, barbaric cruelty by elements associated with the government of North Vietnam. This was not a reading of dry statistics or some scuttlebutt passed on to me. I was an unwilling participant. I saw it; I smelled it; I heard it. I saw the villagers' all too real agony and fear; I heard their weeping and moaning. I was smeared with their blood when I helped to evacuate the wounded. It was a vicious, premeditated action perpetrated in my presence on helpless people I knew. I can remember some of them giving me friendly little pats on the arm during normal day-to-day encounters. It only serves to worsen the painful memory of the suffering they underwent that dark night while I watched.

Maybe it made such a deep impression on me because I was not trained for combat. I know it is an experience I will never forget and it helps me understand why people who saw and experienced much more than I did feel as they do.
~~~

When Trang Sup Burned

What is worse than the impotent rage
When one is trapped, unable to engage
The enemy when he slips in to kill?

You can only watch with furious eyes
As mortars explode and the agonized cries
Of the victims pierce your soul with a chill

That freezes memories that will never melt,
And bares a nerve that still is felt
In those unguarded moments when you're still.

Then the memories start along with the pain
As the smoke and the fire rekindle your brain
Making you live it once more against your will.

The children scream and the old folks weep
And you close your eyes trying to keep
Out the sights that bore in like a drill.

True anguish comes when the enemy has gone,
You're helping survivors, all bloodied and torn...
And, for you, war has forever lost its thrill.

Discontent

Words, empty phrases, brushes with truncated handles and stiff bristles, how can they paint a picture with genuine feeling? Dying flowers mixed in a bouquet with weeds and thistles that contains only dusty decay. I am weary, weary of lies and hypocrisy, smiling lips and empty, gelid eyes. So inured to the vacuous word, 'brother', uttered with all the empathy, depth, and insight of an ampersand, all the warmth of winter in northern lands. Cliques and coteries, tribes and clans; exclusive of differences, stagnant and inbred. The blind leading the ignorant, all happy to be led. Circling in on themselves in a desperate attempt to remain unique while celebrating uniformity and eschewing critique. Why am I trapped in this stifling room? There must be a place where the sun still shines and roses bloom.

~~~

GI Holidays

Twenty-plus years as a single GI sort of took a bit of the luster off holidays for me, particularly Christmas. I was usually hundreds of miles from home and family - if not on the other side of the world - when Yuletide rolled around. I generally wound up nursing a Cuba Libre, a scotch and water or a screwdriver in a bar somewhere if I wasn't working my own shift or subbing for some married co-worker so he could be with his family.

For some reason, I can't remember my first Christmas overseas, but I do remember that I spent my first New Year's Eve across the pond locked in a hotel room in Barcelona. My buddies had introduced me to the delights of marijuana. Mixed with the Cuba Libres, Sol y Sombras, and Lord knows what else I'd been drinking, the demon weed sort of lowered my inhibitions to the point where I was best not seen in public.

So they took me back to my hotel, locked me in, and bribed the porter to keep an eye on me and let me out only if he thought I was sober enough. It wasn't a problem, since I didn't regain consciousness until well into the next day. Imagine this from a guy who went to church every day until he enlisted in the Air Force. Remember, it was the mid-'50s when I enlisted. I joined the service as the prototypical virginal youth, and departed some twenty years later as an archetype of the incipient, cynical dirty-old-man.

Anyway, because of that episode, I missed out on a charming custom that was practiced each New Year's Eve in Spain. As the midnight hour approached, you'd purchase a small cellophane package of grapes, and as the bells tolled midnight, you would eat a grape and kiss a girl each time the bells sounded. I, Of course, was kissing my pillow that first New Year's midnight in Spain; but I never missed another New Year's celebration during my four year tour there.

I spent another Christmas in a tent up on Easy Queen Mountain in Korea in the company of my old radar set from Vietnam. A two-week TDY somehow got stretched to nearly three months. Reason given was that nobody else seemed to have my success at keeping the old UPS-1 on the air. I know it couldn't have been because of my independent attitude. (It would seem that after Viet Nam, I did not suffer fools too gladly...whoever they might be.)

And, so it went: from Mississippi to Montana to Alaska, or wherever I happened to find myself during the Holiday Season. Sometimes I spent Christmas at friends' homes in Stateside places like Finland, Minnesota, sometimes on a frozen Korean mountaintop, sometimes in an old French fort in a jungle, sometimes in a Barcelona bar. But wherever I happened to be, somehow something or someone always reminded me; I was never able to escape the message of the season.

In Korea it was a high-ranking ROKAF officer (I like to remember him as a two-star general, but I think he was actually a colonel sent by the general) who suddenly appeared in the maintenance tent with gift lighters to thank us for our services. He had been told that I was on the mountain alone, and he came all the way up in the snow to give me my lighter personally rather than leave it down below with my crew.

In Vietnam it was a little Vietnamese handyman whose name is long forgotten but who found us a Christmas tree somewhere. Didn't matter that it looked more like a branch than a tree and we had to improvise the decorations. In Alaska, a young Eskimo boy sent me a walrus tooth as thanks for having taught him to bowl during an Open House. Unfortunately, my ex-sister Nia Kuumba, nee Ethel, stole it from me. Sorry, there's no other word for it; she's been light-fingered all her life.

So, once again as the Holiday Season begins anew: Happy Thanksgiving, Merry Christmas, Happy New Year, Happy Hanukkah, Happy Kwanzaa. Peace on all our houses. The same for Easter, Veterans Day, Memorial Day, the Fourth of July and all the others - Peace and Prosperity. (The picture of the 'Motley Crew' at the top of this page was taken in Tin City, Alaska in '73.)
~~~

Cat Ballou and Hanoi Jane

"Hanoi Jane" Fonda just popped up on TV on a game show, of all places. Using impeccable timing, they scheduled her appearance for just before Veterans' Day. Considering her later reputation with Vietnam vets, it's ironic now that her picture, "Cat Ballou" with Lee Marvin and that drunken horse, was the backup flick at Trang-Sup in 1966. When we couldn't get another picture, we'd break out our private copy of "Cat" and watch it again. After awhile, the whole camp could recite much of the dialogue from memory right along with the actors.

Eventually, "Cat" did wear out her welcome and was traded for some other picture, but it wasn't the same and the new back up picture was soon traded also. No other picture really ever took the Cat's unique place. In spite of Ms Fonda's later indiscretions, I'll always remember "Cat Ballou" with great fondness. Actually, Lee Marvin as the drunken Kid Shelleen aboard his apparently equally tipsy horse gave the movie much of its appeal.

When Marvin won the Oscar for his dual role of identical twins Kid Shelleen and the evil Tim Strawn, he gave all the credit to his horse. One quote I'll always remember: Marvin, as the whiskey-soaked Shelleen, put on a stunning, extraordinary demonstration of marksmanship for Cat while guzzling down a pint of whiskey. Then, he all but collapsed in a drunken stupor when the rotgut lit on top of whatever else he'd already drank. One of the other characters wryly remarked, "I've never seen a man get through a day so fast."

It was like the transformation Ms Fonda has had in my recollections of Vietnam; though the picture has a fond spot in my heart, I'm afraid she does not. As Nat Cole and Stubby Kaye sang in the movie, "Cat Ballou, Cat Ballou...she's mean and evil through and through." I still like the picture, though.

We also used to watch that old Vic Morrow series, "Combat," which the SF folks really liked and referred to as OJT; but some light-fingered knuckle head made off with the TV set. It was never replaced, so we had to fall back on such devices as liars' poker, craps, and real poker to divert ourselves. Funny, I can't remember playing pinochle at Trang-Sup, although I played it everywhere else I was stationed.

But, I seemed to have wandered away from Ms Fonda, which isn't a bad thing, so I guess I'll shut up for now. Oh, I did play pinochle in Vietnam, but that was down in Tay Ninh with the crew I'd brought back after I'd PCS'd to the Philippines. I was sent back TDY from Clark to remove the radar after Detachment 7 had been deactivated. Somebody decided that I was perfect to head up the job since I had "experience" in Vietnam and at Trang-Sup, in particular. Lucky me; I was perfectly willing to let somebody else get some "experience." Lord knows there was plenty to go around.

I got stuck in Tay Ninh West for a few weeks waiting for transport out to the PI with the radar. That was during Tet of '68 and we got shelled every day without fail. One of my better TDYs; I would have much preferred to be TDY in Beautiful Downtown Bangkok rather than where I was - be it Tay Ninh West or Tay Ninh City. I will be forever grateful to the kind soul who sent me back to Vietnam because of my vast "experience".

~~~

Military Marriages

I'm not married and never have been. Early on I realized that I was simply not willing to share that much of myself with another person. In the military or out. But especially not while I was in the military. While I'm almost recklessly generous with material things, something deep inside of me backs warily into a cave when someone tries to get too close emotionally.

When I was in 5th TAC and subject to sudden and frequent deployments, there was a popular song that went, "Who's makin' love to your old lady while you are out making love?" Some wag changed that to; "Who's makin' love to your old lady while you are gone TDY?" That applied to us single guys (more so) as well as to a few married folks. It happened to me. Since I was paying the rent, I simply bounced the wench and went and got another one. Not too easy to do when you've got legal papers and kids, or are just simply cohabiting with the same woman for a long time here in the States. Chanting "I divorce thee" three times does not work in Wichita.

I knew that I could never make the deep emotional and spiritual commitment to another person that I believe is necessary for an enduring and mutually satisfying marriage. I like to go where I please and do what I want whenever I want to do it, within reason, of course. People like me have no business being married; unhappily, some of us get hitched anyway. I guess because it's nice receiving trust and love from another person although you have no intention of fully reciprocating in kind. I once gave most of my paycheck to a married guy who had spent payday playing the slots in the club. He was ashamed to go home broke. (To his credit, he never did that again, and he did repay me.)

I believe that Military marriages require a special understanding and commitment from both parties. There are the constant separations and having to pack up and move lock, stock and barrel halfway around the world that being in the military demands. Or you're on an isolated site in Alaska and your wife is back at your last duty station in North Boonieville dealing alone with all the family problems. Sometimes it's just being suddenly called back to duty on alert when the baby sitter's been hired and you and the wife are planning a night out. Then there's the money. Or lack thereof.

I remember a married E5 asking me, back in the mid-70's, if he should consider using food stamps. He was already moonlighting. I told him that there is no shame in swallowing your pride to feed your family. No, thank you; that was not the life for me. You both have got to be really mutually dedicated to a military career - or at least to each other - to stay in the Service long enough to just make enough money to decently raise your family, in my opinion.

That was Alvin (AKA Max) and Kitty Maxwell, a couple I met in Spain. At the time, Max was an E4 medic, and they had three kids. These two people made you want to get married just from being around them. And neither one was perfect, mind you. But they were perfect for each other. Talk about a marriage here on earth that was made in Heaven. I lost touch with them years ago, but I'll bet wherever they are, they're still together and still in love. Excuse me for getting a little mushy and sentimental, but they had the kind of commitment to each other needed for military marriages to endure. (That's Kitty and Max sitting together in the picture above, and me in the checkered shirt. Mercy! Was I ever that young?)

Some day I'll write about the time Kitty chewed Max out for letting me get drunk. Poor Max had nothing to do with my inebriated state, he just found me in a bar and took me home for safe keeping, but Kitty wouldn't let him get a word in edgewise. He was having plenty trouble explaining why he was in that bar in the first place. I wasn't much help; I thought the whole thing was hilarious and Kitty finally ordered me off to bed. Even in my condition, I knew better than to argue.

Note: I just learned that Max has passed on; almost as painful was the news that his marriage to Kitty had ended in divorce, and that Max had remarried. Whatever, I will always remember him with Kitty, the way they were in those happy days in Spain. TPW
~~~

Guilt

Carrying some degree of guilt seems to be almost universal among Viet Nam vets; it was there even in country. I felt it every time a Special Forces patrol left camp while I remained behind in relative safety. I think the Special Forces people themselves felt it in some measure when they sat and listened to the radio as another camp in danger of being overrun fought for its life. What could they do? They wept, they raged in helpless anger as they listened while their friends were wounded or killed. They knew it was not their fault, yet still they felt guilty. They all knew somebody in those camps. I'm afraid that there isn't any answer; if there is one, I'd sure like to find it.

One young man went out on a patrol when he wasn't scheduled to go. He said that he wasn't being paid to sit around camp playing Liar's Dice with the Zoomies. He said it jokingly, but deep inside, he believed it because it was his job to go out. He was that sort of man; they all were.

He got separated from the others during a firefight, and when they found his mutilated body a day or so later, he could only be identified by his dog tags and some personal items that he carried. I guess we all felt a little secret guilt, from the guy who let him go on patrol when he didn't have to down to the people who wished they'd tried harder to convince him to hang around for one more day of Liar's Dice. But really, it was nobody's fault.

I never told my friend Larry how much I cared for him because I felt that if I did, something bad would somehow happen to him. As if my thoughts or feelings could in some way control his fate. It was irrational and illogical, but that was what I felt and that was what I acted on. The man had already been wounded before I met him. I certainly didn't want to be the cause of any bad luck for him. It made perfect sense to me at the time.

How do you explain the survivor's guilt suffered by men who saw constant combat and even sustained wounds of their own? Still, they feel guilty because they survived when many of their friends and acquaintances didn't make it back home. They may have lived simply because of a caprice of fate. A mortar round came part way through the roof right over Valerie Robert, who was asleep in his bunk on Trang Sup. It didn't go off. Fate smiled on him that night. I wonder if he suffers from survivor's guilt today because of his good fortune then?
~~~

Mistaken Identity

At the risk of causing any Grunts who might read this to groan, I have to admit that we had TV at Penthouse/Trang-Sup until some scut stole the set. I've always suspected that it was the work of a Special Forces Colonel who once accused us Air Force types of corrupting his men. The SF troops, using the shaky excuse that it was OJT, admittedly enjoyed watching reruns of Vic Morrow's WW-II action series, 'Combat!'

The Colonel dropped by the camp one day and found himself faced with a small dilemma: how to tell the Army people from the Air Force ones among the men he saw moving about the general area. Everybody seemed to be bare-chested, hatless, shirtless, wearing a tee-shirt and shorts, a tee-shirt and fatigue uniform pants, or some such combination of clothing that did not readily reveal their branch of service. Fortunately, nobody was doing any nude sun bathing.

The Colonel scanned the men in sight and picked out one of the huskier troops, a well-built young man who, if my memory serves, turned out to be our friendly neighborhood Air Force Sky Cop. The Colonel was not amused. Grumbling something about flippin', undisciplined Wing Nuts, he ordered all the Army personnel into full fatigue uniforms.

Needless to say, although the Army (mostly) continued to wear the proper fatigue uniform for a time after the Colonel left, the wool headgear gradually began to disappear again in favor of cooler covers. Even the Special Forces guys got a chuckle out of the Colonel's mini-tempest, although they'd had to suffer a little because of the Air Force's supposed subversive influence on their choice of suitable tropical attire. Personally, I suspect they'd have pretty much dressed that way while in camp even if the nearest airman had been on Tan Son Nhut.

~~~

The Black Demon

I'll never forget the time I scared the beJesus out of a hapless Thai in Bangkok. I wasn't aware of the superstition they had about this soul-snatching Black Demon. One night I was out barhopping, and came up behind this little guy on a quiet stretch of street. I've always walked softly, and I was wearing rubber-heeled shoes, so he didn't hear me approaching from behind him. As luck would have it, I was dressed in a Navy blue shirt, black slacks, and black loafers. I, of course, am rather dark myself.

This poor little guy became aware of my presence and looked up at me just as I drew abreast of him, so I gave him a big, friendly smile and said hello in Thai. He screamed! The man actually screamed! And started pounding the top of his head! I guess it appeared to him that I had suddenly materialized out of thin air. At the time, I didn't realize what the head pounding was about, but it turns out that I was actually being vigorously exorcised.

He obviously thought that his day had arrived and I was some unholy apparition come to suck up his soul. By patting the top of his head and chanting an incantation, he hoped to drive me away. I'm sure he believes to this day that he had the narrowest escape of his life, because although the patting and chanting didn't have any actual effect on me, the scream certainly got me started on my way out his AO in a hurry.

Can you imagine that poor little man's terror when I suddenly appeared in the night, seemingly out of nowhere? At my six foot height compared to his, I must have seemed a giant to his frightened eyes.

I'm sorry I scared him, but I'll bet he behaved himself for a long time after our little encounter. Really taught me another meaning for the term "Soul Man." I can't help but think of Fred Sanford staggering about clutching his chest and calling out piteously for Elizabeth to prepare a place for him, 'cause this was "The Big One."

Then, there's the time I single-handedly invaded Spain early one morning; but that's another story that happened in a far different part of the world.
~~~

Compañeros de Mi Vida
(My Life's Companions)

I wonder what they're doing now,
Those friends from so long ago?
The ones who came to grace my days
When my hair was untouched by snow:

Mullen no longer patrols Michigan's
Roads in his mighty F-86D;
He's probably home in Texas again,
With his imagination not quite so free.

I'll bet he'd be surprised to know
That, a few years later in Spain,
I met a guy named Hooker who also
Drove a Volkswagen fighter plane...

Then there was 'Rat', my amusing friend
With a wit that was rapier keen,
Who was also surprisingly strong,
Though his physique was whippet lean.

His nickname didn't do him justice,
Curtis Mallory was his real name,
And I'm mighty glad he was around;
His humor helped keep me sane.

And clever, smooth-talking Corley,
Who was never at a loss for words,
I'm sure old Ray could solve Bush's
Snafus with Shiites and with Kurds.

There was always a Corley or Curtis
Who somehow seemed to be near
Whenever life took a nasty turn,
Or the skies grew clouded and drear.

From Mississippi to Vietnam, on
The prairie or a high mountain top,
I had the great good fortune to find
The very cream of God's own crop.

So, here's to you, the cherished friends
I met from Cut Bank to Bangkok...
May the music of your lives play on
...May you Forever Rock.
~~~

It seems another old friend pops up every month now. The latest, Rick Rogers, tells me that just recently, he has either seen me looking just as I appeared in '69 - '71, or one of my offspring. I assured him that I haven't been caught in a time warp and I most definitely am not driving a UPS truck in Georgia at this time. I'm not sure if I have any children living there as I have no idea where my oldest son is. He's the only surviving child I have that I know about. Rick says that he sees the man regularly, and the resemblance is so uncanny that he has hesitated to approach him, lest he discover it really is me, unchanged by the years.

Ed Mullen and I used to drive around in his Volkswagen Beetle just for the hell of it. During our adventurous road trips, Ed, who was a radar operator, would assume the dual roles of fighter pilot and intercept director, homing in on various enemy intrusions into our sacred air space. I don't remember if an F-86D had a GIB, but that's the role I filled. Those were more innocent times. Kids today would probably be driving around looking for somebody to carjack instead of pretending to be jet fighter jocks. As I remember Ed, the only civilian clothes he seemed to own were tee shirts and blue jeans. I suppose being from Texas had something to do with that.

'Rat' got his nickname because of a hilarious incident - as he told it - when he was accidentally left behind in Lethbridge, Canada, and had to hitchhike back to the radar site. Never depend on drunken friends for a ride home. In any case, Curtis spent a chilly night in an Amish farmer's barn, jockeying with various livestock for position around a lone space heater. He swore a pig tried to 'Bogart' his coat. 'Bogart' was slang for achieving something without actual force by assuming an intimidating appearance. It comes from movie star tough guy Humphrey Bogart. Curtis claimed the hog threatened to kick his butt if he didn't give up the coat, but mention of rashers of bacon and smoked hams scared the porker off.

By the time Curtis finally made his way back to us, he was a little the worse for wear. Curtis is, or was, a small, slender man, and one of our considerate friends kindly remarked that, in his bedraggled state, he looked like a homeless rat. He didn't smell any too appealing at the time, either. The nickname stuck.

The Hooker (upper case H) in the poem is the only one of my acquaintance, although I have had the pleasure of making friends with any number of the small 'h' ones at various stops on life's journey. Happy times were had by all. The term 'hooker' supposedly came from the last name of Union General Joseph Hooker:

Popular legend has it that his name was permanently attached to prostitutes because of his Civil War actions in rounding them up in one area of Washington, DC. Wikipedia says: Despite Hooker's reputation as a hard-drinking ladies' man, there is no basis for the popular legend that the slang term for prostitutes came from his last name because of parties and a lack of military discipline at his headquarters. Some versions of the legend claim that the band of prostitutes that followed his division were derisively referred to as "General Hooker's Army" or "Hooker's Brigade." However, the term "hooker" was used in print as early as 1845, years before Hooker was a public figure. The prevalence of the Hooker legend may have been at least partly responsible for the popularity of the term.

PTSD...Then and Now

Someone on SafeHaven mentioned concentration camps the other day. I immediately thought of an old friend I had met when I was stationed at Rosas Air Force Station in Spain. Tom was a WW II combat veteran who had survived the Bataan Death March; he was the second case of PTSD I'd seen close up and on a nearly daily basis.

Of course, we didn't call it PTSD then; we called it "Shell Shock" and we just looked the other way when Tom got drunk, which was pretty often, and went on a crying jag or started beating up on the shuffle board game, his only target. He could consume a case of beer by himself and still navigate. Not well, but he usually stayed on his feet until somebody got him to bed. I believe the Air Force allowed him to eventually retire gracefully.

On the other hand, there was my first crew chief, John, also a WW II Army combat vet. He rivaled the famed Audie Murphy when it came to the number of earned combat decorations he was entitled to wear. But the Air Force bounced John out of the service because of his drinking. John was the first person suffering from PTSD that I unknowingly encountered.

John knew his job inside out, and was never publicly violent that I can remember, but the people in his chain of command - which mirrored Tom's - didn't consider his war record or experiences in combat as mitigating circumstances. As a result, John T. was gradually reduced in rank from an E-6 to an E-3, and eventually put out of the service short of retirement. Both men had given full measure to their services and country, but in the end, they were treated differently.

I suppose John's downfall came about because nobody ever bothered to connect his day-to-day drinking with the day-to-day horrors that he'd experienced in combat. They didn't associate his constant state of mellow inebriation with his war service, I suppose because he bore no visible scars. And when he did talk about the war, he made light of it.

I remember him gleefully telling me how he deliberately waited for a clear shot so that he could plink a German soldier in the ass. John cackled merrily throughout the telling as he recounted how the startled man leaped into the air, angrily cursing him in German as he flung his carbine away, and he had me laughing with him. John T. could have nailed the guy with a second shot, but he didn't. Now I wonder how many other memories were roaming through his mind; the ones he never laughingly shared.

To the best of my knowledge, neither Tom or John ever received any sort of treatment or counseling for their condition. As a matter of fact, I'm dead certain neither ever did, at least, not while they were on active duty. It's a pretty good bet that neither received much in the way of counseling or whatever from the VA after they returned to civilian status.

"What have you done for me lately?" has always been the theme once the GI came home from the war and removed his uniform for the last time. And there's little chance that it's going to change any time soon. I would suppose that time has gentled my memories somewhat, but I know that John T. was a good man, and he deserved better from the Air Force.

~~~

Dave Stevenson

Return to Trang Sup

I've been reminiscing about Trang-Sup and 5th TAC. In the spring of '68, I returned to Vietnam to remove the radar from my old site on Trang-Sup. Dear old Detachment 7, 619th Tactical Control Squadron had, alas, been deactivated; tossed on the ash heap of history. Two things must be understood early on: 1 -

I had returned to Trang-Sup under protest; 2 - I do not enjoy driving large, multi-wheeled vehicles under any circumstances. From the moment we picked up the trucks at the motor pool on Clark in the Philippines and up to the point when we had everything loaded and were down in Tay Ninh West waiting to return to the PI, I had exercised my prerogative as package chief and remained a passenger.

When we got to Trang-Sup, we found that the site personnel had already dismantled and packed most of the radar gear. All we had to do was take down the radar tower, pack it up, and load the trucks. Seems the Permanent Party troops were in a hurry to leave Trang-Sup for some reason. Taking down the tower took us a little longer than usual, because I stopped work in the middle of the day and resumed later on when things had cooled off a little. I saw no reason to give anybody heat stroke.

Then, word got passed around that a big attack was imminent, and we sort of speeded things up a tad, but it was too late. We wound up with six heavily loaded six-bys, deuce-and-a-halves, or whatever you want to call them, down on the Army base in Tay Ninh West smack in the middle of the offensive. Charlie took delight in energetically mortaring and rocketing the hell out of the place on a daily basis. He seemed to particularly enjoy firing at the hospital.

At any rate, over the next two weeks or so, we managed to get transport out for each of the trucks, one by one until there was but one left. I told that driver to go on back to Clark with the remainder of the crew and I'd bring the truck back myself on the next available flight. So, I was left with a loaded six-by and the Captain. Our anticipated one day wait for a flight lengthened into another week. By now, our supposed two weeks TDY was rapidly about to pass a month in duration. Finally, the Captain decided that he was going up to Saigon and stand on somebody's desk. "The next time you see me," he declared, "it'll be on the flight out of here."

He then disappeared for about another week, leaving me alone amongst a bunch of strangers with a truckload of radar gear to guard at night by the rockets' red glare and the mortars bursting...well, you get the idea. Fortunately, the Army took pity and continued to feed me. During the day, I slept in the empty rec room that the Army had provided to house my crew. Meanwhile, in addition to the attacks on Tay Ninh West, I had a ringside seat as the VC attempted to overrun the American installation on top of Nui Ba Den. The mountain is clearly visible from Tay Ninh. Indeed, it can be seen for miles from just about any direction.

After about another week of waiting, I'd just about decided that my captain had forgotten about me and returned to the PI alone. Either that or, consumed with frustration, he really had leapt up on somebody's desk and been summarily thrown into LBJ for gross insubordination. I hoped it wasn't the latter, because he was a good guy, and I liked him. Then, came a phone call alerting me that he had gotten us a flight out and would see me shortly.

Soon, here he came, racing into the rec room to tell me that we had about ten minutes to retrieve the truck and get it down to where an aircraft waited. "We've got to get one of the Army guys to drive the truck to the plane, and we have no time to waste!" he panted. "They're not going to wait for us." "Who needs the Army to drive?" I asked, picking up my already packed gear. "Let's get the truck." The Captain looked at me in surprise. "I thought you said you couldn't drive a Six-by." "No, Sir," I replied, "I never said I couldn't, I said I wouldn't. Now, I've changed my mind. Let's go!"

The Captain just shook his head as I chauffeured us rapidly down to the flight line, and backed our limo right up to the plane. I would have backed it on board, but I guess the Loadmaster didn't trust me. "Sergeant Woodfork," the Captain said, "you never cease to surprise me." Little did he know - even if I hadn't known how to drive one of those things, I'd have learned on the way to the plane in order to get away from Tay Ninh and Tet. Mama Woody didn't raise no fools; I'd already done my year's tour in Nam; this crap was extra.

Oh, hell, I nearly left out the best part. When I finally got back to 5th TAC in the Philippines, The Powers That Be informed me that three of the trucks, still loaded with electronic gear, had mysteriously disappeared. (They had all been signed out to me.) Millions of dollars worth of equipment, for which I was responsible, had simply vanished, and they wanted to know what I was going to do about it.

"Well," I said, "first I'm going home and make love to my girlfriend. Then, tomorrow, I'll come back and we can discuss my promotion to five stars so that I can pay for all this shit." How the hell was I supposed to know what had happened to the trucks? I was in Tay Ninh, thousands of miles away, hiding from mortars when the vehicles arrived back on Clark.

They eventually turned up some time later. I forget now exactly what had happened to them. I do know that it was something stupid; somebody had moved them to a different area from where the drivers had parked them as they arrived, one at a time. They were still fully loaded when found.
~~~

Again, the Drums

Now begins that melancholy time that I was so afraid of seeing; war again looms on the horizon with all the attendant pain and horror it brings. As many gloat in anticipated triumph, their children go toward battle and oblivion with constricted breath and racing hearts. They will selflessly give their all for God and country. Others mouth boastful defiance as their children turn to face an irresistible, death-bearing torrent of steel and fire with trepidation and hopeless bravado.

On both sides, youth will cease to bloom. It will wither and die in the consuming furnace of War's fiery breath. Meanwhile avaricious, stony-hearted men wait with grasping hands to reap the bounty provided by the sacrifices of those aborted futures. Somewhere, hopefully, a God notes the actions of these Wicked in His Book of Reckoning.

That, however, provides cold comfort to those who will presently, and for years to come, mourn the empty place at the table and bear that aching void in their hearts. Custom can neither stem hot tears nor protect minds from the decades of pain that await both the victorious and the defeated.

What monument ever restored a heartbeat, breathed warm life again into flaccid, lacerated lungs, caused a new limb to grow, or returned the light to sightless eyes? So, "beat the drum slowly..." the blood chilling rasp of the Grim Reaper's whetstone against his scythe echoes once more. It has begun anew.
~~~

The Deadly Drumbeat.

What a monstrous sight, this picture of America's best casually discarded in an ignominious pile. It burns like a dagger seared through the chest. What is to be gained by displaying human beings like trophies from a safari?

I wonder if the sight of these young people, flung aside like worthless rubbish, has changed the resolve of those remaining who offered to stand as human shields before the perpetrators of this hateful abomination? Some 'shields' have already left in shock after discovering the depth of the depravity of the regime that they had come to protect.

I can think of no surer way to steel the resolve of their fellows to avenge the desecration of these compatriots who fought honorably and were treated so ignobly in death. These were people who had come, not out of a desire to conquer another people, or for personal gain, but because they felt that they were preserving their own freedoms. Or simply because they were following orders.

They did not deserve this. One can only hope that those who are responsible, who slyly pretend to surrender and then attack from behind a white flag, will discover here on earth a measure of the hell that awaits them after death.

I was watching the news - I forget which channel, I surf a lot - and someone called Rep. Charles Rangel, who is advocating a reinstatement of the military draft, a fool. I was deeply touched by the patriotic attitude.

Ah, Patriotism

Have you gone daft?
Bring back the draft?
Nobody's exempt?
I never dreamt...

I support the troops,
but this fruit loop
wants me to be one!
I'm quite undone!

Me, carry a gun
in that desert sun?
What a crock;
you're off your block.

Sorry, my man,
I don't need a tan.
Don't make me laugh;
you *have* gone daft.
~~~

The Way Things Sometimes Are

 Lord, how I miss my trusting youth
When I was so sure I knew the truth;
Those were the days when I knew
Precisely what was honest and true.

Now, older and wiser, I sometimes grieve
For the loss of what I used to believe,
Back when youth was vital and strong
And my ideals would brook no wrong.

Did I go too far; did I see too much?
Has my soul lost that gentle touch
That stayed my hand when anger rose,
And kept me from delivering blows

To sweep opposition from my path
And fling it away in a gust of wrath?
Way back then I could always see
Why folks sometimes disagreed with me.

I had thought patience grew with age;
But, instead there's this silent rage
Hidden deep within my brain
That I must always carefully restrain

So that it can't erupt, destroying me
With everything that I can see.
At times, inside, I am cold and still,
Filled with fury that gives me chills.

And I wait, while my memory plays
Back through dusty, bygone days,
To a dark, frightening, deadly refrain,
To a place where only madness reigns.
~~~

Homecoming

An end to snipers
And IED flak
While patrolling the
Ominous streets 0f Iraq;

Peace and tranquility
Now rule his land;
He no longer treads
The bloody sands.

His time has ended in
The service of the sword;
He sleeps in peace in the
Arms of the Lord.

My son, my child, my
Hope for the future,
His uniform conceals
The surgeon's sutures

That could not stay
His ebbing life,
And return him whole
Again to his wife

And his own sons who
In sorrow weep
Over the coffin where
Their hero now sleeps.

The rifles fire,
The bugles play,
Honoring the end
Of his earthly days.

I turn away, and
Stifle a curse;
I see approaching
Another hearse...

The snipers remain
As does IED flak
For others who patrol
Deadly streets in Iraq.

- For those brave souls who truly stayed the course.
~~~

David Honey

The Dream Renewed

Here's to the enduring spirit of the Fourth of July,
Flags whipping briskly against azure skies,
Dazzling fireworks exploding noisily way up high,
And, somewhere, a soldier dies.

That sacred life should never be spent in vain,
No patriots singing piously of fruited plains
While grasping, venal men reap selfish gain
Shaming our Flag with dishonor's stain.

So many souls come to Heaven's gates,
Having given their all to assure our fate,
Dying so this nation would always be great,
Its citizens standing fearless and straight.

America must retain possession of its soul,
And continue to nourish those spirits bold
Who strive toward that noble goal -
Melding diversity into a harmonious whole.

God grant that glorious dream come true,
Nourished by the Red, White, and Blue,
Where brave, honest folk receive their just due
As they secure our beloved country's dreams anew.

*'O say does that Star-Spangled Banner yet wave
O'er the Land of the Free and the Home of the
Brave?'

*The Star-Spangled Banner by Francis Scott Key.
~~~

Why I Went to Vietnam

Why did I volunteer to go to Vietnam? Thinking
back, I can't come up with a single, cut-and-dried
reason for my decision to go over and actively take
part in the Vietnam War. Idealism, coupled with
boredom and a desire for adventure, in addition to
the realization that I had worn a military uniform

nearly every day of my life for ten years, were all factors. Besides, military people are supposed to fight in wars, aren't they? After all, aggressively waging war is what the military is ultimately all about, the misnomer 'Department of Defense' notwithstanding.

Without doing a lot of analyzing about it, I had chosen the military for a career, and I was on active duty when Vietnam heated up. My country was involved in a war; where else should I have been? There really wasn't any overwhelming sense of patriotism behind the decision. It was another part of the job I had chosen to do. I didn't leave home on a mission with banners flying and trumpets blaring.

Without any braggadocio, I chose not to be an interested observer from a safe distance. I considered it part of my duty to help. My older brother felt the same way; a 'Lifer' like me, he also volunteered to go to Vietnam. We never discussed it and he had already volunteered by the time I made up my own mind to go. It's possible, though, that his decision had some unconscious influence on me.

I don't remember talking about patriotism or about fending off the communist peril while I was, in the parlance of the times, "doin' my thang" in 'Nam. There wasn't much altruistic concern for the plight of the downtrodden Vietnamese peasantry on my part either, at least, not initially. I had never so much as given them a passing thought before arriving in their country. A measure of empathy came later, after I got to personally know some of the people. I did feel sympathy for the cruel toll the war was taking on those locals that I knew. After helping load a few of their bleeding bodies onto Medevac helicopters, I couldn't help but feel sorry for them. With any luck, in a finite amount of time, I would return home to relative safety. This was their home; there was no 'safe place' for them to go.

As far as I remember, nobody serving with me ever asked what the hell I was doing on Trang-Sup. Most of the Americans I knew, both Air Force and Army, were there because they wanted to be there – for whatever reasons, we had volunteered to come. The Army Special Forces people, in particular, had voluntarily undergone long, arduous, specialized training in order to perform their assigned mission. This is what they did, where they wanted to be, and they were admirably well trained and dedicated people.

As for me, except when we were under attack and I manned a machine gun on camp defense, my job as a radar repairman was pretty much the same as it would have been had I decided to remain at that radar site up in the Judith Mountains of Montana. Unlike the Army people on Trang-Sup and elsewhere, my job didn't require that I go out into a hostile environment searching for a cunning and elusive enemy. It was bad enough that Charlie came looking for me.

Of course, off-base life would have been a lot more humdrum in Montana. Nobody would have been lurking around outside the perimeter walls trying to sneak in and murder us as we slept. Nobody would have mounted repeated armed assaults on our compound with malicious, lethal intent. Hopefully, nobody would have occasionally aimed 'Friendly Fire' in our direction. Although at Lewistown, from time to time some apparently myopic hunter back in the woods would fire on the blue Air Force bus as it carried crew changes up and down the mountain between the cantonment area and the topside radar site. Perhaps they mistook it for some weird wild kin of Paul Bunyan's ox. Also on the plus side, the sanitary conditions in Montana were vastly superior.

In any case, there I was at Detachment 7 of the 619th Tactical Control Squadron, located on Trai Trang-Sup, Tay Ninh Province, South Vietnam, in the area designated as War Zone C in III Corps. After a few months, I inevitably began looking forward to getting my tour of duty over with and going back home in one piece with all my parts still attached and in reasonable working order. A few of my compatriots, bless their dedicated souls, did decide to extend their tours. I respected that decision. I also declined to join them.

Life in Vietnam was dangerous, noisy, nerve-wracking, and, for the most part, it smelled pretty bad, to boot. People got wounded and maimed, and they got killed, violently and a lot more messily than in those war movies I'd seen. Life in Vietnam was also, at times, just boring. No other way to describe it. Those were the times when absolutely nothing was going on and there was no place to go, especially during monsoon season. And, I had never in my life imagined I'd ever consider 75°F to be cold. Certainly not when I was still in northern Montana. The boring part was more like life was for me on that mountaintop.

During the early part of my military career, I served with veterans of both WW-II and Korea, and I had heard words like 'shell shock' associated with World War II and the 'Korean Conflict'. Despite having once been stationed with a survivor of the Bataan Death March and Japanese POW camps, I really wasn't fully cognizant of the grievous and enduring mental wounds war can inflict on many of its participants. I'm much more aware of that aspect of war now. Like many physical scars, the evidence isn't always readily apparent.

That's it; more than a little simplistic, I know, but there's no mystery, no hidden reasons, no search for glory. I wanted to see what war was like. I also believed that I had some real obligation to be involved in it, so off I went to both do my duty and see war at first hand for myself. It was both more and less than I had expected.

In the end, I found out what real war is like. I definitely have decidedly mixed feelings about John Wayne now.

~~~

©2001 T.P. Woodfork Det. 7, 619th TCS, 1966-1967

Guitars, Sandbags, and Saigon Tea

Sitting on the sandbags watching the war,
Wondering what on earth I volunteered for.
Hearing Larry's guitar softly play, while
Pondering just what I've accomplished today.

Riding in a cyclo down Tu Do Street,
Watching ladies in Ao Dais, clean and neat,
Gliding by bar girls with sirens' eyes
Offering Saigon Tea and enticing thighs.

Smelling burnt flesh, a bitter stink,
Seeing young-old eyes that never blink.
Listening to White as he pats his feet
Strumming his guitar while keeping the beat.

Hearing my voice singing soft and low
Snarling folks back home yeling, "I won't go!"
Sitting down on the end of my rack
Thinking 'bout the ones who won't come back.

Staring at the tracers, neon bright,
Searching for a life to snuff tonight.
Crouching behind sandbags fighting the war
Knowing now exactly what I volunteered for:

Preserving the right of the people to be free
To spit on the Flag, this uniform, and me.
~~~

Big Skies and Rice Paddies

Just thinking: I don't remember the day I arrived
in Viet Nam. Neither is there much memory of
the long, long, transoceanic flight from
California to Saigon. I remember that I did come
alive with the excitement of being in such a new
and exotic place; and of course there was the
added fillip of the threat of sudden death.

I don't clearly recall the day I arrived,
But I do remember that I came alive
At the prospect of death being so near.
And oddly enough, there was no fear.

But I wasn't really afraid. While at thirty-one
years old, I didn't have the blissful conceit of
youth's belief in immortality, death was still
something that happened to other people.

That came later, with the first attack
When it dawned on me I might not get back
To grumble about Montana's 'Big Sky'
That had spread before my citified eyes.

That changed with the first attack, when it
became inescapably apparent to me that there
really were people who, although they had never
met me, were determined to help me shuffle off
this mortal coil. All that, and crotch rot, too.

There was something about a bullet's hum
That made me realize this wasn't much fun,
And, maybe in Biloxi, it got just as hot,
But at least I never suffered from crotch rot.

Believe it or not, there were actually times when I felt a bit of nostalgia for the grand sweep of 'The Big Sky' country. Even if I was only half joking when I said I volunteered for Viet Nam to escape Montana. Those visits to Glacier National Park did have their good points, even for this city boy.

"You can only watch with furious eyes
As mortars explode and the agonized cries
Of the victims pierce your soul with a chill
That freezes memories that will never melt,
And bares a nerve that still is felt
In those unguarded moments when you're still."

I don't remember the flight out of Saigon, either. Coming and going, both a complete blank. A lot of what happened in between those two events has also vanished from my memory as though it never was. But I do remember Viet Nam. Yes, I do.

I don't remember boarding the flight,
I don't recall what was my last sight
Of the land that has so affected me;
Now why, do you suppose, that should be?
~~

Index

Page

PHOTO CREDITS

Photos:
David Honey
Lymon Rigby
Faye Sizemore
Dave Stevenson
Thurman Woodfork